STORIES FROM
AMERICAN HISTORY

MYRTIS MIXON

National Textbook Company
a division of NTC/CONTEMPORARY PUBLISHING GROUP
Lincolnwood, Illinois USA

Acknowledgments

I'd like to thank these people for their help.

Randall Imel for his unflagging encouragement.

Alma Flor Ada for her help as my advisor in the doctoral program at the University of San Francisco,

Jeffery Breyer who is willing to proof-read, field-test, and even do the dishes.

Michael Lacapa for reading and commenting on the story about Chief Joseph.

Virginia, Greg, and Christine Collins for taking me to the "Fountain of Youth."

Barbara Budge Griffin for her inspiration as a storyteller.

Arabella Simon for field-testing the stories.

Dottie Imel for giving me interesting story ideas.

These people helped by reading and discussing the stories: Casey Gardner, Rita Kanell, Dawn Tankersley, Suzie Pharr, Mildred Dauterive, Mary Thibodeaux, Katherine Taylor, Louise Pederson, Rachel Collins, Arabella Siman, Nancy Mixon, and Mary Burns.

Photo Credits

The following credits also apply to the corresponding chapters in the timeline on pages iv and v.

Pages 2, 58, 66, 82: Brown Brothers

Pages 10, 18, 26, 34, 114: The Granger Collection

Pages 42, 50, 74: Culver Pictures

Page 98: ©H.L. Shantz/U.S. Forest Service

Page 106: AP/Wide World

ISBN: 0-8442-0445-5

Table of Contents

**Mark Twain and
the Gold Rush
(1862)**

**Pocahontas:
In Two Worlds
(1607)**

**Johnny Comes Marching
Home Again
(1865)**

**Dolley Madison and
the War of 1812**

**Ponce de
Leon and
the Fountain
of Youth
(1513)**

**The Witches
of Salem
(1692)**

**1867: The Chinese Strike
Against the Railroad**

1500   1550   1600   1650   1700

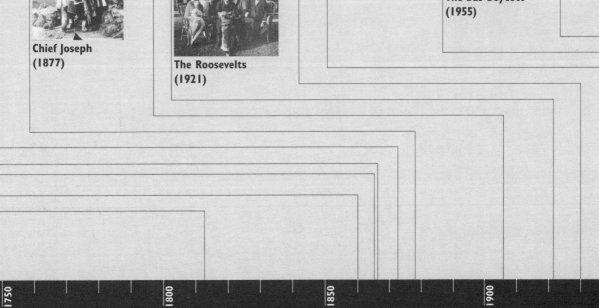

**The Arrest of
Susan B. Anthony
(1872)**

**The San Francisco
Earthquake of 1906**

**The Magic of Disney
(1930)**

© Disney Enterprises Inc.

**The Web of Life
(1940)**

**Protesting the
Vietnam War
(1968)**

**The Bus Boycott
(1955)**

**Chief Joseph
(1877)**

**The Roosevelts
(1921)**

1750   1800   1850   1900   1950

Chapter 1

Ponce de Leon *and the* Fountain of Youth

BEFORE YOU READ

Answer the following questions.

1. Do some older people try to look younger? How? Why?

2. If you were alive at the time, would you sail with Columbus to find the sea route to India and China?

Words to Understand

Read the sentences. Discuss what the words in **boldface** mean.

Words About the Discovery and Exploration of New Lands

1. Brave men **explored,** or traveled, looking for **treasure:** gold, silver, jewels.
2. The explorers made many **voyages,** trips, looking for treasure.
3. They **searched,** or looked for, **spices** too.
4. At first the **natives,** people living there, were friendly.
5. When the natives **attacked,** they **shot arrows** at the Spaniards.
6. Ponce was the **commander** of his ship.

Words About Water

1. Ponce de Leon searched for a **spring,** one that **bubbled** from the ground.
2. In a large **bay,** water protected from the ocean waves, the men **waded,** or walked in the water.
3. They filled the **barrels** with the water that smelled like **sulfur,** a chemical.

Active Vocabulary Learning Activity

Work in pairs on a word or phrase your teacher gives you. Try to show or illustrate it. For example, if your phrase is "shoot arrows," you can say the phrase and at the same time make the physical motion of "shooting an arrow." If you wish, you can also make some gesture or facial expression related to the vocabulary.

Finally, repeat the word or the phrase and action with the class. Here are the words to use in this story:

explore, spring, disappoint, bubble, search, wade, attack, barrels.

*B*ecause Europeans wanted tea and **spices** from India and China, they needed an easier, shorter way to get there. In the 15th century, the water route around Africa was long, and the land route was dangerous. They wanted a shorter water route. Christopher Columbus believed the world was round. Therefore, he said, if he sailed west from Spain, he would reach China or India. At that time, Europeans didn't know a great piece of land lay west, between Europe and China. Columbus, looking for China, found parts of this land. Twenty years later, Juan Ponce de Leon, who had sailed on Columbus' second voyage, landed on North America. He **explored** Florida in 1513. On this **voyage,** many believe he also looked for a Fountain of Youth.

Ponce de Leon and the Fountain of Youth

Looking for Youth

"Is there really a Fountain of Youth?" Ponce de Leon asked his friend Ovando.

"It sounds unbelievable," said Ovando, "but if it is true, old King Ferdinand would love this kind of **treasure**. You would be a hero if you found such a thing."

5   "Yes, that treasure would be greater than gold or new lands. Then I would be **famous** among explorers."

Ponce prepared to sail. With three ships he planned to explore islands north of Puerto Rico.

All Spanish explorers searched for gold. But Ponce wanted more. He want-
10 ed to find the Fountain of Youth. Many islanders said that the magical fountain was on Bimini, the Indian name for the northern land. They said a **spring** was there, and if one drank the water or bathed in it, one would never grow old.

A week before the voyage, a **native** boy named Bori came to see the **commander.** "My father and uncle left 10 years ago, looking for this Fountain
15 of Youth. My uncle returned, looking no older than when he left. He said they had found the magic fountain. Please, Commander, let me go with you to look for my father."

"Bori, bring your uncle to me." Ponce said.

"Sorry, sir. My uncle died of **small pox** a few weeks after he returned."

Land of Flowers

20 "Then how can we find your family?" asked the commander.

"My uncle gave me this map." It wasn't a good map.

They sailed in March 1513. They sailed through the Bahamas. They saw no land for several days. On March 27, Easter Sunday, they saw a **bay.** They landed in this bay where the city of St. Augustine, Florida, is now.

25   The land was beautiful. Flowers were everywhere: magnolias, jasmine, gardenias, honeysuckle — such sweet smells. Ponce de Leon planted the Spanish flag, naming the land *Pascua Florida,* Spanish for "Easter of Flowers".

    Ponce and Bori looked for a spring. The soldiers looked for gold and pearls. Ponce sent his servants inland to look for pools that looked different in any way,
30 more flowers on the banks, more animals drinking from it, anything unusual.

    On the second day Bori came running. "Sir, come to this spring. It's different." A large pool **bubbled** from an underground spring. Ponce took off his **metal** coat of armor and **waded** in. He drank a hatful of water. It tasted and smelled like **sulfur.**

35   Could this be the famous one? He bathed in it and drank glass after glass. Bori swam in the pool but got out quickly, afraid the water would keep him a boy.

The Magic Water

By midafternoon, Ponce felt relaxed and renewed. He was convinced that this <u>was</u> the famous fountain. They camped beside the spring. The next morning,
40 after a two-hour bath in the pool, Ponce went back to the ship. "Ovando, this is it. I've found it. Unload the empty **barrels,** we will fill them with water to bring to the king."

    "Ponce, how do you know this is the spring?" asked his friend.

    "Friend, can't you see it in my face. I feel younger already, after only 24
45 hours."

    "Perhaps," thought Ovando, "perhaps he looks better, the lines around his eyes are a bit softer." Ovando didn't want to **disappoint** his leader.

    Ponce went to his room to get his mirror. "Surely I look younger already."

    The men carried the barrels to the spring. Ponce sent them away to look for
50 gold while he took his afternoon bath.

    Everyday Ponce spent hours in the pool and drank and drank the water. Every morning he looked into the mirror, each day finding more signs of returning youth.

    Everyday the Spaniards looked for gold and pearls.

55   But Ponce was interested only in the water. He filled the barrels with the sulphurous water. He planned to bring it back to old King Ferdinand. Too bad this water is too late for Queen Isabella, he thought.

"Am I younger?"

On the seventh morning, the soldiers came to Ponce at the fountain. "Sir, there is no gold here. We want to move on." Ah, thought their leader, I have
60 found gold of a different sort here. I am ready to go. I have my precious gold in barrels.

    They sailed south. At the next bay, they saw **natives** on the shore. Ponce landed, bringing gifts of knives, fishing hooks and bells, things made of metal. These natives spoke an unknown language, but they made signs they would
65 return with food.

    Ponce and Bori waded up the river, looking for another magic spring. The sailors sat on the beach. They dreamed of palm wine, coconut milk, rich foods, beautiful women.

guᴈmã. mıchᴠácã.

Like the Carib, the Aztecs also fought the Spaniards.

Instead the natives **shot arrows** at them from trees. They **attacked** the
70 Spaniards. Outnumbered, the Spanish hurried to their ships.

Ponce and Bori heard the noise. The angry natives were between them and
the ships. "The ships won't leave without us." said Ponce. "Unless Ovando
thinks we're dead." That night they swam to the ship. The men had waited for
their captain.

75 This attack changed Ponce. It made him look older. All the youthful feelings from the baths in the spring began to **wear off.** But he kept drinking the
water anyway. At least it gave him hope, and he knew it wouldn't hurt him.

Importance

The story of Ponce's **search** may be true or not. No one knows for sure. Many
believe he was the first explorer of the North American continent. He named
all of the continent for Spain, so in early maps, the whole continent was called
"Florida." A few years later, he went on a second trip to Florida. This second
trip was to make a permanent settlement. His ships carried carpenter and
farming tools, horses, cattle, pigs and seeds. They landed on the west coast of
Florida, thinking there were no natives there. They were caught by another
surprise attack. Ponce de Leon was hit in the leg by a poisoned arrow. He died
a few days later. He is remembered not for finding a continent, but for his
search for eternal youth.

Focus on the Story

1. Understand the Story

Finding the main idea. Circle the best answer.
1. This story is about
    a. the Spanish explorations in the Americas.
    b. one Spanish explorer's search for a fountain of youth.
    c. the discovery of America by the Spanish.
2. In this story Ponce de Leon is shown as
    a. a man who wants to believe there could be a cure for old age.
    b. too stupid to be a commander.
    c. unkind and heartless toward his men and the natives.

2. Practice Vocabulary

Choose the word or definition that is closest in meaning to the word(s) in **boldface.**

disappoint	natives	attacked	wearing off
spring	small pox	metal	famous

1. The natives **shot at** the Spaniards.
2. Ovando didn't want to **displease** de Leon by saying Ponce didn't look young.
3. The magical quality of the water was **going away slowly.**
4. The **water coming up from the ground** smelled like sulfur.
5. The uncle caught **a contagious disease.**
6. The **people who had always lived there** didn't want the Spanish to land.
7. The Indians usually liked things made of **a hard substance,** like knives and bells.
8. Ponce became **well-known** for finding Florida and looking for a Fountain of Youth.

3. Understand Details

Find the incorrect word in each sentence. Cross it out and write the correct word(s) at the end of the sentence.
1. The Spanish explorer Ponce de Leon was looking for China.
2. A man gave Ponce de Leon a map to find the fountain.
3. Ponce's ship landed in Virginia.
4. When these Spaniards found St. Augustine, they were looking for farmland.
5. Ponce knew that the natives liked presents made of wood.
6. Ponce's ship left him after the attack.
7. Ponce said the water was good for nothing.

4. Talk About It

Discuss these questions with a partner or in a small group:
1. What were Ponce de Leon's big dreams besides finding a fountain of youth?
2. Why was the water too late for the queen?
3. Why did the Europeans explore the American continent?
4. How did the natives act toward the Europeans coming to their land?
5. Why did Ponce think he'd found the fountain of youth? Do you think he had found it?
6. Discuss why people look for lasting youth. Explain what you understand about this.

5. Write What You Think

1. You are Ponce de Leon. Write a letter to your wife in Spain.
2. Write a physical description of the beautiful spring, the flowers, and everything about the Fountain of Youth.
3. Write about the problems between the natives and the Europeans.

6. Play the Part

Choose a situation below. Plan a dialogue between the characters and act it out.
1. **Ponce, Ovando.** Ponce persuades Ovando to look for the Fountain of Youth.
2. **Ponce, Bori.** Bori persuades Ponce to take Bori with him on the voyage.
3. **Ponce, Ovando.** Ponce tries to convince Ovando that he has found the Fountain of Youth.
4. **Ponce, female native.** Ponce tries to get more information about the area and the fountain.
5. **Ponce, other Spaniards.** Men talk Ponce into leaving his special bubbling spring.
6. **Spaniards, natives.** Spaniards ask about gold and pearls.

7. Geography Focus

1. On Map 1 trace the two routes the Europeans used to travel to China in 1492.
2. On Map 2 show where Ponce de Leon went on his two trips.

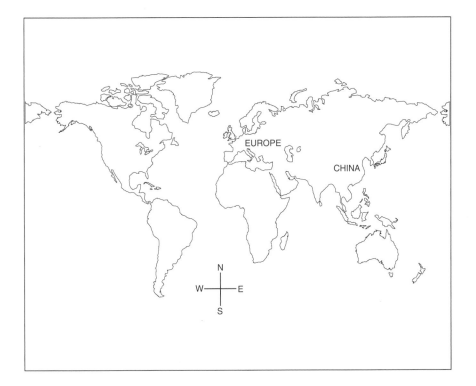

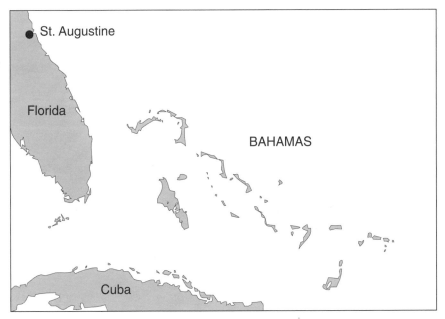

Chapter 2

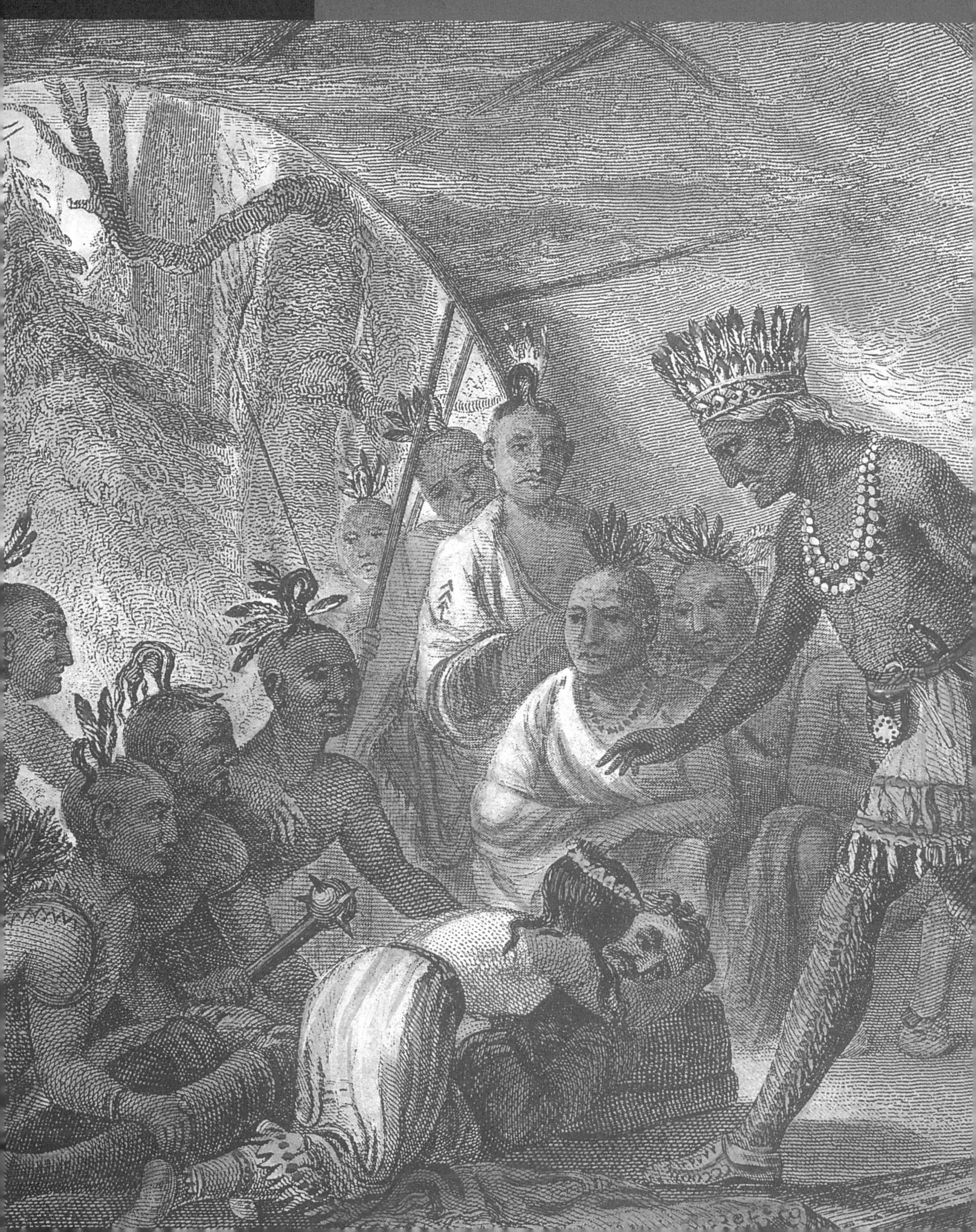

Pocahontas: In Two Worlds

BEFORE YOU READ

Answer the following questions.

1. How would you feel if new groups came to your land to stay?

2. What do you know about Pocahontas?

3. What do you know about Native Americans?

Note: The people of the Americas have been mistakenly called "Indians" for centuries. Many Native American people prefer being called by the name of their tribe, for example: Cherokee, Carib, Hopi, Apache, Nez Perce, Dakota.

Words to Understand

Read the sentences. Discuss what the words in **boldface** mean.

Words About Native Americans
1. Chief Powhatan wore a **robe** of animal skins.
2. Powhatan **adopted** Captain John Smith as his son.
3. Pocahontas said that her people adopt their **enemies** as a way of making peace.
4. Pocahontas **went back and forth** between her people and the English.
5. **A big feast was served** to all the people.

Words About the English in the New World
1. The English wanted to **establish colonies,** to **settle** in the 'New World.'
2. Smith couldn't understand their language, but they **seemed** to be saying no.
3. He thought she was **praying** for, asking for, his life.
4. At one time, the English didn't have enough food; they were **starving.**
5. The **nanny** didn't like the boy to **interrupt** her story.

Words About Fighting
1. The natives **captured** Smith and took him to the court of Powhatan.
2. Smith said, "Many men **dragged** me to the stones, and **raised their clubs.**"
3. Powhatan did not **trust** the Englishmen.
4. Smith was strong and always **survived** when people tried to kill him.
5. The English **kidnapped** Pocahontas and held her captive in Jamestown.
6. This did not **break the will** of Powhatan; he did not **give in** to the English.

Active Vocabulary Learning Activity

Work in pairs on a word or phrase your teacher gives you. Try to show or illustrate it. For example, if your phrase is "shoot arrows," you can say the phrase and at the same time make the physical motion of "shooting an arrow." You can also make some gesture or facial expression related to the vocabulary.

Finally, repeat the word or the phrase and action with the class.
Here are the words to use in this story:

> captive, dragged, back and forth, kidnap, raise the clubs, interrupt, robe, praying.

*A*fter Columbus went to America, other European countries wanted to **establish colonies** too. The first English colony was in Virginia. Captain John Smith was part of the group that **settled** Jamestown in 1607. His meeting with Pocahontas is the subject of poems, stories, and films. He wrote an account of their meeting, and his part of this story is based on Smith's account. Some historians do not believe Smith's account, the popular story of Pocahontas saving Smith's life. Here we give the story from two points of view: Pocahontas and John Smith. It is introduced by Thomas, the son of Pocahontas and an Englishman.

Pocahontas: In Two Worlds

A Story for Thomas

"Tell me the story again, nanny. Tell me about my mother."

"Your mother was a great Indian princess. Her name was Pocahontas."

"I know that part. Tell me about how she saved Captain John Smith."

"I have to start at the beginning. Your mother was the daughter of the great
5   Chief Powhatan, and they lived in Virginia."

"Was that before my father went to Virginia?" asked Thomas.

"Do you want me to tell you the story? Stop **interrupting** me, dear Thomas."

"Tell me the story from the beginning."

10   "There are many beginnings, but I'll start with Captain Smith's story, and then I'll tell your mother's story. Captain Smith and his men **settled** in Jamestown in 1607. They went there hoping to find gold, and a way to get to India and China too."

John Smith's Story

I am Captain John Smith. After living in Virginia for a few months, my
15   soldiers and I started exploring the area. We were looking for the ocean that would take us to India and China, but suddenly we were attacked by natives. They killed all my soldiers, but seeing that I was the leader, they took me **captive.** They took me to a great long house.

Their chief, the great Powhatan, was there with more than 200 men stand-
20   ing around him. Powhatan sat upon a great bed, covered with a **robe** made of animal skins. People were lined up on both sides of Powhatan: in front were two rows of men, and behind them were women, with their heads and shoulders painted red. Many had white bird feathers on their heads, and great chains of white beads around their necks.

25 When I went before this chief, all the people shouted. A queenly woman brought me water to wash in, and feathers to dry myself.

A big feast was served, and then they talked for a long time. I couldn't understand their language. After the feast they placed two great stones in front of Powhatan.

30 Then many men **dragged** me to the stones and laid my head on them. They all had **clubs in their hands,** and I thought they would beat my brains out.

A young female came running to me, from way across the room. She talked a lot, perhaps **praying for** my life. Everyone **seemed** to say no to her. The

35 woman put her head on my head, as if to say that they would have to kill her at the same time. She was willing to save my life by giving hers, or to die with me.

This saved me. The young woman was Pocahontas, the daughter of the chief. He **adopted** me. He took me into his house, and I made him hatchets, bells and beads.

40 After two days he told me I could return to Jamestown, but I should send him two great guns and a grindstone, and I would be his son, Nantaquoud.

Captain John Smith

Pocahontas' Story

I am Pocahontas. I was happy to save Captain Smith. This is what we do, adopt the leaders of our **enemies.** I was glad to have a white brother. I hoped we would all live in peace.

45 My father, Chief Powhatan, **does not trust** the white men. He says, "The white men lied to me and killed many people. Now there are more white men, near the great water, the ocean." My father does not like white settlers and does not want them to live on our land.

I liked John Smith. He taught me his language: *gun, wife, coat, friend.* I

50 taught him our language. I was glad to give him and his men corn and to help them. I was happy to **go back and forth** between these two worlds.

I wanted to live in both worlds, but now I know those worlds are too different. My people don't want the English people on our land, but my people want their guns, and they will take the guns if the English don't give them to

55 us. The English want food from us, but mostly they want gold, and they want to make money on our land.

I wanted peace, but it wouldn't last. My people and the English fought many times. Captain Smith took some of my people captive. I brought a deer as a gift, and Captain Smith let the captives go. There was peace again.

60 Many years passed this way: first there would be peace, then fighting, and then peace again. Many of my people wanted to kill John Smith, thinking that the English would leave then. They tried to kill him but he always **survived.** Perhaps he had some magic.

My people tried to kill the settlers, but more came. After three years here

65 Captain Smith went back to England for a rest. The English told us that he was dead and buried.

Once he was gone, my people were less afraid, so they tried to kill all the settlers. The settlers were afraid to go into the forest, afraid of being killed by the Powhatan people. The white people didn't have enough food because they

70 still couldn't farm. This was called the "**starving** time." They were hungry and sick. Many died.

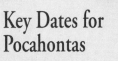

They were eating horses, dogs, even mice and rats.

I was afraid for the English, so I took them baskets of corn and asked my brother to bring them small animals. At this time, 1610, I was 14, old enough
75 to marry and I married Kocoum.

New settlers came, and the colony of Jamestown started all over again. The new leader, Captain Argall, asked Powhatan to return guns and captives. Powhatan said, "Let the English get out of my country."

But they didn't, and by 1613, there were more than 700 settlers, 30 of
80 them women. I was living in the Potomac country. The English captured me, **kidnapped** me. They hoped to **break the will** of my father, Powhatan.

My father was not worried about me. He knew they would not hurt me. In Jamestown they taught me how to live the way they did. They forced me to go to church and study the Christian religion.

85 Because I always felt close to the settlers, it wasn't hard for me to live with them. I missed my people. I'm not sure why I didn't run away.

After a while, I met an Englishman named John Rolfe. We married and had a son, my Thomas. Then we went to visit England. I think I still thought that I could help the English to know and **respect** my people.

90 In England I became famous. I had a new name, Lady Rebecca Rolfe. But I didn't want to live there. I wanted to go home.

———————————

"Nanny, what happened then?" asked Thomas.

"Oh, Thomas, that is the sad part. Your mother was never able to return home. Your father, your mother, and you left London; but before the ship
95 sailed for Virginia, she got sick with smallpox, a "white man's disease." She had to get off the ship, and she died in England."

Key Dates for Pocahontas

1595 Born in what we now call Virginia, daughter of a tribal chief, Powhatan

1613 Captured by Captain Argall and held by the settlers; took the name Rebecca

1614 Married English settler John Rolfe

1615 Gave birth to her only child, Thomas

1616 Went with her husband to England, became famous, and met the king and queen

1617 Died in England of smallpox while waiting to return to Virginia

SOURCE: Brown Brothers

Pocahontas, as Lady Rebecca Rolfe, with her son

Importance

Without the help of the tribal peoples, the first settlers in the New World would not have survived. Pocahontas became a symbol of a native that helped the English. Stories and now films give us confusing, perhaps untruthful, images of her life in both worlds. We don't have anything written in her words to know what she felt.

Focus on the Story

1. Understand the Story

Making your own questions. Go through the story, section by section, and make 10–15 questions about the important ideas in this story. Do this alone, in a pair, or in a group of three. Afterwards, you can pass the questions to another person or group and see if they can answer them.

> **Example:** Why did the English settle in America?
> Why didn't Powhatan trust the English?

2. Practice Vocabulary

Use these words to complete the sentences:

dragged	feast	interrupt	survived
enemies	kidnapped	colonies	did not trust

1. The nanny didn't want Thomas to _____ during the story.

2. The English wanted to establish _____ in the New World.

3. The natives served a big _____ to their guests.

4. The natives _____ John Smith to the large stone.

5. Pocahontas was _____, taken captive, by the English.

6. Powhatan _____ the English because they lied to him.

7. Powhatan saw the English as _____, not friends.

8. John Smith _____ every attack. He lived through everything.

3. Cause and Effect

Complete each sentence by choosing the right cause. The first part of the sentence is the effect, the end result.

Example: John Smith explored the area because
   a. he was looking for food.
   (b.) he wanted to find a route to India and China.
   c. he was looking for Pocahontas.

1. The English settled in Virginia because
   a. they wanted to convert the natives to Christianity.
   b. they wanted to make money from the New World.
   c. they liked the climate.
2. Chief Powhatan did not trust the English because
   a. he said they lied and killed people.
   b. they had guns.
   c. they wanted to find a route to China.
3. Peace between the English and the Native Americans could not last because
   a. they were natural enemies.
   b. they didn't speak the same language.
   c. they wanted different, conflicting things for the land.
4. Pocahontas was kidnapped (captured) by the English because
   a. they thought it would break the will of Powhatan.
   b. they wanted her to marry an Englishman.
   c. they wanted to kill her.

4. Talk About It

Discuss these questions with a partner or in a small group:
1. Do you know other stories or films about Pocahontas? How are they different from this one?
2. Did the English have any moral right to the New World land?
3. How did Pocahontas and John Smith see the world differently?
4. If you were Captain John Smith, how would you keep the peace with the Indians?
5. Why is Pocahontas such a popular, almost legendary, character?

5. Write What You Think

1. Write a version of this story from the viewpoint of either John Rolfe or Chief Powhatan.
2. Write a few days' entries in the journal of a Jamestown settler, in 1607 or 1610.
3. You are a newspaper reporter, in England or elsewhere in Europe in 1608. Write about the settlement in Jamestown.

6. Play the Part

Choose a situation below. Plan the dialogue between the characters and act it out.

1. **Pocahontas, John Smith, Powhatan.** Pocahontas wants to save Smith; Powhatan wants him to die.
2. **Pocahontas, her brother.** She wants to help the English; he doesn't want to.
3. **Pocahontas, an English soldier.** He kidnaps her; she resists his capturing her.
4. **Pocahontas, her father.** Pocahontas wants to help the English more; Powhatan refuses.
5. **Pocahontas, John Rolfe.** He asks her to marry him. She says no; she must be true to her people.
6. **Pocahontas, the queen or king of England.** The queen or king wants her to stay in England. She wants to go back home.

7. Artistic Response

On a piece of paper, draw a picture, cartoon, story in sequential pictures (a storyboard), or a mind map, responding to this story. Use any kind of visual response to the story that you can imagine. Then take turns explaining your "art" in small groups or to the class.

Chapter 3

The Witches of Salem

BEFORE YOU READ

Answer the following questions.

1. **What is a witch? Do you believe they exist?**

2. **Do you know about any witch hunts in history, anywhere in the world?**

Words to Understand

Read the sentences. Discuss what the words in **boldface** mean.

Words About the Legal System

1. The girls said old Sarah was a witch. They **accused** her of being a witch. The officer put her in **jail;** she couldn't go home.
2. Then there was a **trial,** and she was **convicted** of the crime of witchcraft.
3. Many women were **suspected,** under **suspicion.** If an accused woman **confessed,** she would not be **executed,** not be killed.
4. After being convicted, the accused witches were **hanged.**
5. One woman got away, **escaped** to New York.

Words About Strong Emotion

1. The girls were **bored,** tired of doing what they did everyday.
2. The witch hunt started when the girls **screamed** and **yelled** about witches. Sometimes they **swooned,** looked semiconscious as if they might faint.
3. The girls said they could **recognize** the witches, would know them.
4. Mercy wanted the witches to confess so that they wouldn't hang. Old Sarah wouldn't confess. Instead, she **cursed** Mr. Hathorn, saying he would be hurt by God. Mercy said Sarah was **stubborn,** not easy to control or deal with.
5. Later, Mercy felt **guilty** about hurting so many people.
6. Goody Kary said the Putnams were **greedy;** they wanted more land.

Popular Words from the 17th Century

1. **Goodwife,** or **Goody,** and **Goodman** were used instead of *Mrs.* and *Mr.*
2. The **devil** is the name of the most **evil** creature, the opposite of God.
3. **Mistress** refers to a female employer or owner; a word of respect.
4. The **Puritan** religion controlled everything. The **minister** had great power.

Active Vocabulary Learning Activity

Work in pairs on a word or phrase your teacher gives you. Try to show or illustrate it. For example, if your phrase is "shoot arrows," you can say the phrase and at the same time make the physical motion of "shooting an arrow." If you wish, you can also make some gesture or facial expression related to the vocabulary.

Finally, repeat the word or the phrase and action with the class.
Here are the words to use in this story:

hanged, bored, escape, scream, curse, yelled, stubborn, serious, swoon.

"Witches are here" was the cry, and the madness started. In 1692, in Salem, Massachusetts, a strange and terrible thing happened. The Puritans, a religious group, believed the **devil** worked through human beings called witches. The madness began when Tituba, a slave woman from the Caribbean islands, told stories about witches and magic to some young girls. The adults found out, and the girls got scared and said Tituba was a witch. As the gossip about 'witchcraft' increased, the girls pointed at other women and said they were witches too. Before it was over, more than 200 people had been **accused** of witchcraft, 141 jailed. Nineteen people and two dogs were tried, **convicted,** and **executed.** Most of them were women. Two others accused died in prison, and one man was hurt so badly that he died. Mercy, one of the young girls doing the accusing, tells this story.

The Witches of Salem

The Witchhunt Begins

I ask myself why the witchhunts started. Maybe because we were **bored.** All we ever did was sew, make butter, bake bread, wash and iron clothes, say Bible lessons, and go to church. We never played. Then Tituba, a slave, told us stories about witches. She told our future by dropping egg white into a
5 glass. I asked, "Who will be my husband?"

Tituba was fun. With her, we played games, even dancing at night in the trees. Abigail, Betty, Ann—we did that for months before the grown-ups found out. The dancing was the most fun, but we knew that wasn't **allowed,** so we didn't tell them.

10 Everything changed when Betty got sick in church. She **screamed** and rolled on the floor. I don't know what was wrong with her. She even tried to fly. When Betty did that, people said, "Witches are in Salem. Who is the witch doing this to Betty?"

I was working for **Goodwife** Elizabeth and **Goodman** Nathaniel Kary
15 as their housemaid. Abigail, the oldest of us girls, came to see me. She said that we must go to a court meeting in Salem. "Mercy, you must agree to everything I say. If you don't, I will say you danced **naked** in the dark." That scared me.

I went to **Goody** Kary. " I must go to Salem to a meeting tomorrow."

"But Mercy, it isn't Sunday. You cannot have a day off. You must help me
20 here. I need you to build the fire, bake the bread, milk the cow, and watch the children."

"Goody Kary, the **minister** calls us girls to court in Salem. I can't do the housework now. I am called. It is **serious.**" Suddenly I felt important.

Mercy is 'possessed' at the trial.

"I will not help the devil."

The meeting was **serious.** Then they brought in poor old Sarah. Abigail
25 started **yelling,** "Stay away from me. I will not do the work of the **devil.**"
We looked at Abigail, then we **imitated** her.

"Stay away, old Sarah, I will not do the work of the **devil,**" all of us girls
repeated what Abigail said.

Abigail yelled, "Don't make me do bad things."

30 We **swooned** and sang in chorus, "Don't make me do bad; don't make
me do bad." Abigail went on her hands and knees, barking like a dog. Ann
Putnam, Betty, and I yelled and rolled on the floor. Everything was crazy.

From that day on, we were the center of attention. "You girls must come
to court every day because you can **recognize** the witches," said Mr. Hathorn.
35 He knows everything about witchcraft. "A witch's power comes from the **devil.**
She gives her soul to the **devil** and he gives her what she wants," he said.

Goody Kary didn't want me to go to court, but Abigail said, "Goody Kary,
those against the court are under **suspicion.**" Abigail was the leader of the girls.
She could call anyone a witch, and the court would believe her.

40 The court **accused** and **convicted** many people I knew. Many of them
were good people. Some were hanged. People were convicted of witchcraft if
Abigail said they were witches. She yelled about a person, "She hurts me. She
bites me. She pulls my hair." We repeated, "She hurts us. She bites us. She is
with the **devil.**"

Some People Confess

If they **confessed** to being witches, they weren't **hanged.** I wanted them
to give in. But many were **stubborn,** and they were **hanged.** The only way
to **escape** hanging was to confess. Fifty confessed. Tituba confessed. They
all lived.

Old Sarah wouldn't confess. Right before being hanged, she **cursed**
Mr. Hathorn. "You are a liar. I am no more a witch than you are. If you kill
me, God will give you blood to drink." We were all there watching. It made
me sick to watch her die.

Ann Putnam and her mother accused a saintly woman, Rebecca Nurse.
Abigail accused her too. Abigail threw herself on the floor. She beat her head.
She kicked and screamed "Stop it, Goody Nurse. You hurt me. You stick
pins in my belly. I won't do bad for you." Abigail swooned. I swooned too.
I swoon when Abigail swoons.

My mistress **Goody** Kary said the trials were **evil.** "Mercy, the Putnams are
using you girls. They want more land. People tell stories to hurt neighbors."
"That can't be. No one is that **greedy.** No one kills others for more land."
Her words made me think. But when I got into the court, I did what Abigail
did.

Then today it changed for me. The witch **trials** turned bad for me today.
Ann Putnam accused my **mistress,** saying, "Elizabeth Kary came to me last
night and asked me to sign the devil's book." Before I knew what I was doing,
I was calling my **mistress** a witch.

When I heard myself saying "**Goody** Kary is a witch. She comes to me
in the night. We do bad things," something happened in my head. When they
put her in **jail,** I started shaking. What had I done? I had put my good kind
mistress in **jail.**

The Great Escape

The Karys had been good to me. I went home. Captain Kary said, "Mercy,
you must help my wife. She will die if we don't help," he said. "Mercy, we
must save her."

"Everything's crazy now. What can I do?" I asked Captain Kary.

"Elizabeth isn't a witch. They will hang her if you don't help. Two hundred
people have been accused of witchcraft; 141 have been jailed. Four more witches were convicted and **executed** this evening, bringing the number to 14.
How can you be part of this?"

I cried for an hour. I swooned, almost the way I did in the court. I began
to see things differently. I said, "I won't be part of it anymore. I see the truth
now. It started as a game. We did it for "sport." I'm so sorry, but what can I do?
What will the court do to me if I cry out against the girls? They will call me a
witch. I know it."

"Mercy, don't go to court tomorrow. I'll tell them you are sick. I have a plan."

I slept better that night than I had for weeks. No witches visited my dreams.

The next night the captain and I went to the **jail.** The jailer was at the inn
eating dinner. Kary walked into the **jail,** broke the lock to his wife's room, and
freed her. We ran to the water and rowed to a ship in the bay. We sailed away.
She was safe.

Everyone in Salem came out to watch the hangings.

90   I live in Rhode Island now. Captain Kary and Elizabeth live in New York. I still feel **guilty** about what I did. Nineteen people were hanged because of us. Others died in **jail.** Why did we do it?

Importance

No one knows why the witchhunt in Salem happened. This witchhunt was the largest in America, but these hunts had been common in Europe for 300 years. This one marked the end of witchhunts in Europe and America. The witchhunts served to make women more submissive and fearful, because women were the usual target of the witchhunt.

Focus on the Story

I. Understand the Story

When did this happen? Put the story events in order by placing the correct number 1–8 in the blank. The first event in the story is chosen for you.

_____   Mercy sees the truth and wants to help Goody Kary.
_____   Betty gets sick in church, and the witch hunt begins.
_____   Goody Kary is named a witch.
___1___   The girls read the Bible, sew, cook, clean. They are bored.
_____   Many people are arrested, convicted, and hanged.
_____   Captain Kary and Mercy help Goody Kary escape from jail.
_____   The girls call out the names of many people, calling them witches.
_____   Tituba, the slave woman, tells stories about witches to the girls.

2. Practice Vocabulary

Choose the word or definition that is closest in meaning to the word(s) in **boldface.**

recognize	serious	escape	were greedy
were allowed to	naked	evil	imitated

1. We never **got to** play. We never **got to** dance.
2. Finding witches was not a joke, it was an **important** event.
3. The girls **copied** everything that Abigail said.
4. Goody Kary had to **run away** or she might be hanged.
5. To kill someone for more land is a **terrible** thing to do.
6. The Putnams **never had enough** and wanted more and more land.
7. Abigail said Mercy danced **without clothes** at night.
8. The judge said the girls would **know** the witches.

3. Understand the Characters' Problems

Read about Abigail's problems and solutions; then fill in the missing problem or solution for Mercy and Captain Kary.

CHARACTER	PROBLEM	SOLUTION
Abigail	1. The adults are asking questions about the girls' behavior.	1. She starts "crying out" about witches.
	2. She worries Mercy may not support her.	2. She warns Mercy that she will say Mercy danced naked.
Mercy	1. She wants to go to court.	1. She tells Goody Kary that she must go.
	2. She realizes she has been wrong.	2. _____ _____
	3. _____ _____	3. She says she is sick.
Captain Kary	1. _____ _____	1. He asks Mercy to help.
	2. He wants to rescue his wife.	2. _____ _____

4. Talk About It

Discuss these questions with a partner or in a small group:
1. According to Goody Kary, why does Ann Putnam name Rebecca Nurse as a witch?
2. Guess what Abigail's reasons were for starting the "crying out"?
3. If you lived at a time like this, what would you do? Would you see the truth? Would you help those accused?
4. If you were accused of witchcraft, would you confess to save your life, or would you tell the truth, say you were not a witch, and risk being hanged?
5. Do you know of any events in history that are similar to the witch trials?

5. Write What You Think

1. Write a letter to Mr. Hathorn telling him what was wrong with what he did.
2. Write a short newspaper article about the hangings in Salem.
3. Write about any of the discussion questions in Section 4 above.
4. Write a summary of this story. Use all the main ideas.

6. Play the Part

Choose a situation below. Plan a dialogue between the characters and act it out.
1. **Mercy, Tituba.** Mercy asks about her future; Tituba tells her.
2. **Abigail, Mercy.** Mercy disagrees with Abigail about Goodwife Kary.
3. **Mercy, Goodwife Kary.** They argue about the trials.
4. **Mr. Hathorn, Rebecca Nurse.** He says she is a witch; she defends herself.
5. **Abigail, Mercy, Ann Putnam.** Abigail tells Mercy and Ann what to do; they disagree.
6. **Captain Kary, Mercy.** He argues and persuades Mercy to see the truth.

7. Story Theater

1. Work with a group of students.
2. Choose a section of the story with the class.
3. Read the section with your group. With your group decide which role you will play. If possible, change the whole story to conversation. Feel free to change the description to conversation. Choose any props you wish.
4. Practice your section for 15–20 minutes with your group.
5. Perform your story for the class. Try to make the story theater flow from one part to the next.

Chapter 4

Dolley Madison *and the* War of 1812

BEFORE YOU READ

Answer the following questions.

1. How can a president's wife help him to be a good president?

2. During a war, is it all right to burn the enemy's cities?

Words to Understand

Read the sentences. Discuss what the words in **boldface** mean.

Words About War and Nations

1. James Madison wrote the **Constitution** for the new United States.
2. Madison **declared war** on the British.
3. The noise of the **cannons,** big standing guns, was heard from miles away.
4. The **messenger** brought the news about the invading army.
5. The British **invaded** Washington, the **capital city** of the United States.
6. Dolley Madison said the British leader had **insulted** the nation by saying "I will dine tonight with Dolley Madison in the **mansion.**"
7. Dolley said "Our **private property:** furniture, books, clothes, cannot be saved, **must be sacrificed.**"

Words About Social Life

1. Dolley was **setting the table** for 14 people.
2. Washington's **portrait** was **nailed to the wall** and couldn't be removed.
3. The parrot Willy wanted Dolley to give him more **attention.**
4. Dolley wanted to pack more, **just in case** they could get another wagon.
5. Take this **precious cargo,** these valuables, to my sister's house.
6. Dolley was famous for wearing **turbans** around her head.

Words About Emotion

1. Dolley was **determined** to save Washington's portrait.
2. When Willy sang **"hurrah,"** Dolley said, "Stop making noise, **hush!"**
3. "Writing to my sister **calms me down,"** said Dolley.
4. The Americans thought the British **were being punished** for burning Washington.

Active Vocabulary Learning Activity

Work in pairs on a word or phrase your teacher gives you. Try to show or illustrate it. For example, if your phrase is "shoot arrows," you can say the phrase and at the same time make the physical motion of "shooting an arrow." If you wish, you can also make some gesture or facial expression related to the vocabulary.

Finally, repeat the word or the phrase and action with the class. Here are the words to use in this story:

> hurrah, setting the table, hush, nailed to the wall, attention, invading, messenger, calms me down, insult, turbans.

*D*olley Madison was the popular, attractive wife of James Madison, the fourth president of the United States. This story focuses on the most dramatic day in Dolley's life. At this time America was at war with Great Britain. In 1812 President Madison **declared war** on Britain because they hurt America's shipping and commerce. In this third year of war, British ships entered Chesapeake Bay and came up the Potomac River toward the **capital city,** Washington. On August 24, 1814, Dolley waited for her husband, but about noon it became clear that 3500 British soldiers were **invading** the city. Only 500 American soldiers were there to protect Washington, so these soldiers left. Hurriedly, Dolley packed important papers and other precious things from the presidential **mansion.** This story is unusual because it is told by her pet parrot, Uncle Willy.

Dolley Madison and the War of 1812

The British Are Coming

"The British are coming. **Hurrah.** Hurrah. The British are coming. Hurrah."
I sang out as loud as I could. We heard the noise from the guns far away.
"Willy, now you **hush,** or I'll put you in your cage, and cover it up," Dolley said to me. I was sitting on her shoulder. She was **setting the table** for 14.
5 "I'm getting ready for dinner. The president will come with his generals."
"The British are coming. Hurrah. Hurrah." I liked the sound of that old song.
"That isn't funny. Get down. I'm too busy to carry a silly parrot around,"
she said to me. I hopped onto the table in front of George Washington's big
portrait. I don't get on the floor because I can't be near that bad old dog,
10 King George.
"Madame, may I help?" asked Paul Jennings, the young slave who took care of the house.
Dolley stopped suddenly, "Listen to that **cannon.** It scares me. Paul, would you play music on your fiddle during dinner? The table is ready. Perhaps I'll
15 pack more, **just in case** we have to leave."
"What do you want me to do next?"
"Yesterday, we sent the most important papers—the Declaration of Independence, the **Constitution,** the treaties, to houses in Virginia. What else should we pack?"
20 "Mrs. Madison, how much can you put in your carriage?"
"Not much, but I'm hoping that someone will send a wagon, and then we can bring more."
"The British are coming. The British are coming." I wanted some **attention** and I wasn't getting any.
25 "Uncle Willy, don't you understand? This is war. And we may have to run away for our lives. Oh . . . Willy, I know you can't understand."

Epigrams (special sayings) from this war:

Don't give up the ship.

Our country right or wrong.

We have met the enemy, and they are ours.

She always says that to me. I hate it. I <u>can</u> understand. I started singing
my hunger song, "Time to eat. Time to eat. I know it's time to eat. The bell is
ringing noon."

30 "Oh, darling Willy, I'm sorry. I forgot to feed you this morning. Sukey, get
some of Willy's favorite seeds and bring them in here. He can eat in the sitting
room today. I don't want to be alone," said Dolley. Sukey, a young slave
woman, ran to the kitchen for bird food.

For two days Dolley had packed papers, boxes and boxes of them. She ran

35 from room to room but often found herself at the upstairs windows with her
spy glasses, looking for the British army. "Oh Willy, it's the **fate** of women to
watch and wait."

No Dinner Party Today

Shortly after the bell for 12 o'clock, a **messenger** rode up to the **mansion.**
"Mrs. Madison, Mrs. Madison. General Armstrong has told the army to
40 leave the city. You must leave too." The messenger rode away on his horse.

"Well, Uncle Willy. No company today. No dinner party." Dolley knows
I like company as much as she does.

"John, where are you?" Dolley called for French John,
the main servant in the house. He came in, followed by that
45 smelly old dog George.

I started squawking, "The devil is here. The devil is
here." The dog started barking.

"**Hush,** everybody," said Dolley, and the way she said it
silenced both of us. "Oh, John. I hate to go. I am **deter-**
50 **mined** not to leave until I see Mr. Madison safe. What if he
came here to look for me and I wasn't here! He may be in a
battle right now."

"But Madame, all your friends are gone. It is not safe
here anymore."

55 "If I stay here, maybe I can save the house," said Dolley.

John said "I heard that the cruel British Admiral said, 'I
will dine in Dolley Madison's dining room this very
evening.'"

"That's an **insult** to the nation."

60 "You must not be here if he comes," said French John.

Dolley said, "If we must go, we must take the most
important things, but we cannot take our furniture and
most of our clothes. All our **private property** must be
sacrificed."

65 I flew upstairs with Dolley, and I saw her packing some
of her beautiful clothes and her colorful **turbans.** Dolley is famous for the turbans she wears on her head. She didn't want to be caught with nothing to wear.
Passing through the dining room, she stuffed things in her bag: some pieces of
silver, her favorite clock, even some books. All this work made me sleepy.

70 I woke up from my nap as the bell rang 3 o'clock. The dog, old stinky
George, was nowhere to be seen, but I could hear the guns louder now, Boom!
Boom! Sukey stood by, saying "Madame, how can you be writing at a time
like this?"

Dolley's turbans began a fashion trend.

"It **calms me down.** I'm telling dear sister Lucy that we are still here, even
with a battle nearby, within the sound of the cannon! Mr. Madison comes not;
may God protect him! Two dusty messengers **bid me fly,** but I wait for my
husband."

George Washington Must Be Saved Too

"Look, Madame, another messenger is here," said Sukey.

Paul came running in with the message, "The soldier said that President
Madison says you must leave at once."

My poor Dolley started crying. "What to do? I can't leave everything."
I started making my sad noise. She came over to the table and kissed me,
and then looked up at the picture above me. "Paul, call John. We can't
leave General Washington's portrait."

I squawked as they stood on my table. "Time to go. Time to go. I know
it's time to go." I repeated for all to hear.

John said, "Mrs. Madison, the portrait is **nailed to the wall.**"

"I'll work on it," said Paul. Sukey stood on the table, helping Paul get the
nails out. "It looks impossible," he said.

"The British are coming. It's time to go. The British are coming," I repeated,
but I left off the **hurrahs.** Everyone was so upset, they might get angry with me.

"We must save this one picture of the father of our country," said Dolley.

"I'm afraid I cannot remove the nails," said Paul.

"Here's an **ax.**" said John. "Mrs. Madison, I believe we must break the frame."

"Yes," said Dolley. "Break the frame. We'll take the picture without it."

"Madame, another wagon has just come to help us," said Sukey.

"Thank God. Now, we can take my favorite crimson-red velvet draperies
from my sitting room, and the East Room's eagle ornaments, the leather books,
and four more boxes of presidential papers." said Dolley.

To the wagon driver she said, "Take this **precious cargo** to my sister's
house in Maryland."

I Stay Behind

Dolley knew she would be one of the last to leave the city, but still she took
another minute to write a final word to Lucy. "It is done. . . . When I shall
again write you or where I shall be tomorrow, I cannot tell."

When the carriage came, Dolley turned to me. "Uncle Willy, John will take
you to the French Ambassador. The British won't hurt you there." Maybe, but
their cat might.

"Dolley, don't leave me. Dolley, don't leave me." I always say this as she walks
out the door.

"Uncle Willy, don't break my heart." She was crying. She was crying for me.
She and Sukey climbed into the carriage with all their boxes. They waved good-
bye to us and then rode onto Pennsylvania Avenue, crossing over into
Georgetown.

"What about me? What about me?" I said to French John.

He picked me up. "Don't worry, Uncle Willy. You'll be all right."

After all is said and done, I was the last to leave the mansion. Does that
make me a hero?

Dolley was not going to leave the mansion without Gilbert Stuart's full-length portrait of George Washington. In this picture he stands tall in a black velvet suit with lace at the throat and wrists, standing by a scarlet-covered table, one hand gripping a sword, the other outstretched.

At nine o'clock in the evening, the British marched to the Capitol building, seated themselves, and in good humor voted to burn down the city. At 10:30
120 they went into the mansion and drank some of the wine, took what they wanted, and then set the mansion afire. The fire light could be seen 40 miles away.

The next morning, almost like a punishment for the British, a giant storm came into the city and put out the fires. A giant wind came in, pulling up trees, unroofing houses, overturning cannons. A falling wall killed 30 British soldiers.
125 They retreated to their ships, and the Madisons returned to Washington.

Importance

Although James Madison was the person most responsible for the writing of the **Constitution** in 1776, in his later years as president, he wasn't always popular. He was **criticized** for his actions during the War of 1812 against the British. Many people say that without Dolley he would not have been reelected in 1812. Dolley was James Madison's greatest good fortune, and America's most popular First Lady. She was charming and hospitable and kind, but she was also a woman of substance. Dolley had the three gifts necessary to a happy life: much to do, much to love, and much to hope for.

Focus on the Story

I. Understand the Story

Find out. Read the question. Find the answer in the story. Write it on the line.

> **Example:** Why does President Madison declare war on Britain?
> <u>The British hurt American shipping and commerce.</u>

1. Who is Willy? _____

_____

2. Why is Dolley packing up things in the mansion? _____

_____

3. Who are Sukey, Paul, and French John? _____

_____

4. Why doesn't Dolley want to leave? _____

_____

5. What happens to the capital city after Dolley leaves? _____

_____

2. Practice Vocabulary

Use these words to complete the sentences:

criticized	be sacrificed	fate	insult
determined	invading	just in case	attention

1. The British soldiers were _____ the capital city of Washington.

2. The _____ of women is different from that of men.

3. Something bad said to hurt someone is called an _____.

4. Willy liked to have Dolley's _____ all the time.

5. James Madison was _____ for the way he fought the war.

6. Dolley wanted to pack more, _____ the British did invade the city.

7. Dolley was _____ to stay in the mansion until her husband came.

8. The Madison private property had to _____. It could not be saved.

3. Cause and Effect

Complete each sentence by choosing the right cause. The first part of the sentence is the effect, the end result.

Example: Dolley Madison was so popular because
a. she had a lot of money.
(b.) she was charming, hospitable, and kind.
c. she saved George Washington's portrait.

1. The city of Washington was burned because
   a. the British wanted to punish the Americans.
   b. Admiral Cockburn was an American.
   c. there was an earthquake, and it started a fire.
2. Dolley's furniture and most of her clothes had to be sacrificed because
   a. she couldn't put it all on the wagons they had.
   b. she didn't like them anymore.
   c. her servants were lazy and didn't want to help her.
3. Uncle Willy liked to stay on the table because
   a. his feet got cold on the floor.
   b. he didn't want to be on the floor where the dog was.
   c. he was angry with Dolley.
4. Dolley wanted to save the portrait of Washington because
   a. it was worth a million dollars.
   b. she had painted it.
   c. she didn't want the picture to get into the hands of the British.

4. Talk About It

Discuss these questions with a partner or in a small group:
1. What reasons can you think of that would cause Britain and America to go to war?
2. Why did the British set fire to the capital city?
3. Why do you think that Dolley Madison was so popular?
4. Why did someone good, like Dolley, have slaves?
5. Is it OK to do something that you may think is bad, when everyone is doing it?

5. Write What You Think

1. You are a reporter in Britain. Write an article about the British burning the American capital city.
2. Write an account of this day from Sukey's viewpoint.
3. Write a character description of Dolley.
4. Write a summary of this story. Include all the main points.

6. Play the Part

Choose a situation below. Plan the dialogue between the characters and act it out.
1. **Dolley, Willy.** Willy is telling Dolley why she should take him; she refuses.
2. **Dolley, an American officer.** She argues that she must stay in the mansion. He says she must leave.
3. **French John, a British officer.** They want to burn the mansion. John says no.
4. **Paul, Sukey.** He wants her to marry him. She says no.
5. **Dolley, James Madison.** He wants to resign. She says no, he shouldn't.
6. **French John, Dolley.** She wants to stay to protect the mansion. He says she must go.

7. Story Theater

1. Work with a group of students.
2. Choose a section of the story with the class.
3. Read the section with your group. With your group decide which role you will play. If possible, change everything to conversation. Feel free to change the description to conversation. Choose any props you wish.
4. Practice your section for 15–20 minutes with your group.
5. Perform your story for the class. Try to make the story theater flow from one part to the next.

Chapter 5

Mark Twain *and the* Gold Rush

BEFORE YOU READ

Answer the following questions.

1. Have you ever heard of Mark Twain? What do you know about him? Who was he?

2. What do you know about the Gold Rush to California?

3. What do you know about the western part of the United States in the 19th century?

Words to Understand

Read the sentences. Discuss what the words in **boldface** mean.

Words Connected with the West
1. The stagecoach **sped** across the **flat plains** until it reached the mountains.
2. After **bouncing** on the **steep trails** in the mountains, the coach crossed the **desert.**
3. Mark Twain went west for excitement, **adventure,** and wealth too.
4. A new religion, the **Mormon** Church, was centered in Utah. **Mormon** men originally could have more than one wife.

Words About Mining and the Gold Rush
1. Many miners were **ambitious** and saw the Gold Rush as an **opportunity** to get rich.
2. Nevada was a **territory,** not yet a state.
3. **Mica** looked like gold to the ignorant, thus it was called "Fool's Gold."
4. Samuel Clemens found pieces, **fragments,** of rock that looked like gold.

Descriptive Verbs
1. In the Army, Mark Twain learned to **retreat,** go away from, not toward, the war.
2. Mark Twain gave in, **succumbed,** to the "silver fever."
3. He **sneaked away,** so that the others would not see him.
4. He **crawled** on the ground, looking for gold or silver.
5. The hard work of mining made his dreams of wealth **vanish.**
6. He **teased** his friends, telling them a little, but not the whole story.

Active Vocabulary Learning Activity

Work in pairs on a word or phrase your teacher gives you. Try to show or illustrate it. For example, if your phrase is "shoot arrows," you can say the phrase and at the same time make the physical motion of "shooting an arrow." If you wish, you can also make some gesture or facial expression related to the vocabulary.

Finally, repeat the word or the phrase and action with the class.
Here are the words to use in this story:

> bounce, speed, complain, succumb, frenzied, sneak away, crawl, vanish, retreat.

*A*fter gold was discovered in California in 1848, people from all over the world rushed there for **adventure** and fortune. Then, in 1858 silver was discovered in Nevada. One young adventurer who went west was named Samuel Clemens (1835 – 1910). Later, he used the pen name Mark Twain and became America's most famous writer. He wrote many books; perhaps the best is *The **Adventures** of Huckleberry Finn.* Twain wrote about his own life in several books. Born in the state of Missouri, near the Mississippi River, his boyhood **ambition** was to be a pilot on a riverboat. He succeeded in becoming a pilot, but then the Civil War ended riverboating for a while. He joined the army briefly (two weeks) but was happy to leave the war area and go west with his brother to Nevada. Out west Sam Clemens became a writer and adopted Mark Twain as a pen name. The following story is based on his adventures in the west.

Mark Twain and the Gold Rush

A Stagecoach Trip

I didn't like being a soldier in the war between the North and the South. War and killing aren't for me. For two weeks I was a soldier, but **retreating** was all I learned.

5   I decided to join my brother Orion on his trip west. Orion had been chosen to be the secretary of the new Nevada **territory,** and I became the secretary to the secretary.

Before the railroad, the fastest way to travel out west was by stagecoach.

SOURCE: Corbis-Bettmann

We went by steamboat from St. Louis to St. Joseph, Missouri. From there I paid $300 for two tickets to Nevada on the Overland Stagecoach. In July 1861 we covered 1,700 miles, stopping only to eat and change horses.

10 We traveled 20 days and 20 nights to get to Carson City, Nevada. For three weeks we **bounced** along in the stagecoach, across the **flat plains,** and then we crossed the Rocky Mountains over **steep trails.** We slowed down in the dust of the **desert.**

Adventure was king. At this time the railroads and telegraph had not 15 reached out west. There was danger from Indians and robbers, but we went fast, and the driver had a gun.

We **sped** westward at 8–10 miles per hour behind six fast horses. Sitting in the stagecoach with the other men was pleasant: smoking and telling stories, we were comfortable amid the bags of mail. I told stories about what I would 20 do with the gold and silver that I expected to find out west.

During our stopover in Salt Lake City, Utah, I met the head of the **Mormon** religion, Brigham Young. In one of our conversations, Mr. Young **complained** 25 about the problems of having 97 or more wives. He said if he gave one wife a simple present, such as a "breast pin," it ended up costing him a thousand dollars. Every other 30 wife came in and demanded a breast pin too.

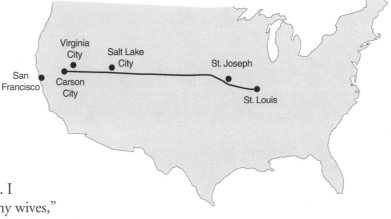

"Married life can be a perfect dog's life. I believe it's not a good idea to have so many wives," said Mr. Young. "It would be better to have no more than 35 10 or 11."

The Terrible Desert

The only part of the trip that I didn't enjoy was the 68 miles of **desert.** We covered the first 45 miles during the night—not so bad; but the next morning, we couldn't go more than two miles an hour. The stagecoach wheels sank in the dusty sand, and the sun beat down. There was no moving air, no clouds, 40 no birds. We ran out of water, and the thick flying dust stuck to us. It was tiresome and dull.

Once we got to Carson City, I heard stories of poor men becoming millionaires overnight. Everyone talked of silver in the hills, sudden wealth, lost mines, and great expectations. The storekeepers were certainly getting 45 rich. They sold flour for one dollar a pound, a loaf of bread for five dollars, a blanket for one hundred dollars. I heard about one hungry miner paying five dollars for a biscuit.

After a few weeks I couldn't help it; I caught the "silver fever" too. As I later said, "I would have been more or less than human if I had not gone 50 crazy like the rest. I began to believe the silver stories after seeing wagonloads of solid silver bricks arrive from the mills every day. I **succumbed** and grew as **frenzied** as the craziest."

I headed out for the silver area with three other men, one an older man, Ballou, who knew something about mining. It took us 15 days to get to the silver city of Unionville. We carried 1,800 pounds of provisions and mining equipment.

The first day in Unionville, I expected that I was going to gather up, in a day or two, or at the most a week, enough silver to make me wealthy.

At the first **opportunity** I **sneaked away** from the group to do a little "prospecting" alone. I began my search with excitement and expectation, sure I would find something valuable. I **crawled** about the ground, examined bits of stone, blew away the dust, and looked at the stone with anxious hope. Soon, I found a bright **fragment,** and my heart jumped! I hid behind a tree and rubbed it to make it shine. The more I looked at it the more convinced I was that I had found the door to fortune.

Gold and Silver Everywhere!

I marked the spot, and carried away my treasure. I looked for more. Of all the experiences of my life, this secret search in silverland was the nearest to perfect happiness. By and by, in the river I found a deposit of shining yellow bits, and my breath left me. It must be gold.

I looked around to be sure no one was watching me. Then I went to the river, and for an hour I looked for more of these gold bits. When it got dark, I returned to the camp with my treasure.

I didn't immediately tell my partners. I just asked them, "What did you find?"

Mr. Ballou, the old miner, said, "Nothing yet. It's fair enough here, maybe, but **overrated.**"

"So you think we'd better go somewhere else?" I asked.

"Not yet," the three men said.

Then I began to **tease** them with "What if we found a mine that would give us $200 a ton? Would that satisfy you?"

"Tell us more," they all said.

"What if we found a mine that would give us $2,000 a ton? Would that satisfy you?"

"What do you mean? Tell us more," they all said.

"What if someone told you that right down there, near this spot, there are piles of pure gold and pure silver, enough to make us all rich in 24 hours?" I yelled.

"I would say 'that someone is crazy,'" said old Ballou, but he was excited too.

Fool's Gold

"Well, gentlemen, I don't know anything, but look at this and this and that," and I spread my treasures before them.

They jumped for the treasures, and looked at them closely.

Then, very slowly, old Ballou said, "This isn't gold and silver. I'm sorry but it is nothing but worthless rocks and glittering **mica** that isn't worth 10 cents an acre."

Out west, Sam Clemens found another world

*T*he country is fabulously rich in gold, silver, copper, lead, coal, iron, quicksilver, marble, granite, chalk, thieves, murderers, desperadoes, ladies, children, lawyers, Christians, Indians, Chinamen, Spaniards, gamblers, coyotes (pronounced Ki-yo-tees), poets, preachers, and jackass rabbits.

—FROM *Roughing It*

95 My dream **vanished.** My wealth melted away. I said, "All that **glitters** is not gold."

But Ballou went further and said, "Nothing that glitters is gold. Gold in its natural states is dull uninteresting stuff."

My lesson was that I treat men this way too— **underrating** men of gold 100 and glorifying men of **mica.**

True knowledge of the nature of silver mining came fast enough. For a few weeks we worked with pick and shovel and then dynamite, but we found nothing of great worth. Few men found much gold or silver; even fewer got rich.

Back I went to Carson City. For two years I looked for wealth in the mines. 105 I wrote long letters home about my western **adventures.** They were printed in the newspapers back East, so I sent some letters to the *Territorial Enterprise* in Virginia City, a rich mining town. The *Enterprise,* the best paper in the West, printed them too.

One day, Orion said, "Sam, you've got a letter from Virginia City."

110 I read the letter aloud: "'Please come to work for us as a reporter. We offer you $25 a week.' That doesn't sound bad at all," I said.

"That surely is more than you make as a miner," said my brother.

I walked the 100 miles to Virginia City to become a newspaper writer.

Soon, I started using my pen name, "Mark Twain," words from my river days, 115 that meant "safe water."

Samuel Clemens as a young man.

SOURCE: The Granger Collection

Importance

The discovery of gold and silver in the West brought many fortune seekers. Many people who didn't get rich stayed anyway to become settlers, farmers, or storekeepers. Mark Twain didn't stay. After becoming famous as a writer in San Francisco, he went back east, and made money by writing and giving lectures. He used many of the stories he gathered out west to amuse millions in his audience. Samuel Clemens was born when Halley's Comet appeared in 1835 and died when the comet returned on April 21, 1910. He had predicted that that would happen.

Focus on the Story

1. Understand the Story

Making your own questions. Go through the story section by section and make 10–15 questions about the important ideas in this story. Do this alone, in a pair, or in a group of three. Afterwards, you can pass your questions to another person or group for them to answer.

Example: Why did Samuel Clemens (Mark Twain) go out west?

2. Practice Vocabulary

Use these words to complete the sentences:

ambition   complained   frenzied   overrated
glitter   teased   vanished   opportunity

1. Gold doesn't _____ in its natural state, but mica is shiny.

2. Men went west for adventure and the _____ to get rich.

3. Sam only hinted at what he had found; he _____ his partners.

4. It took energy and _____ to go out west to look for fortune.

5. Some silver towns were _____, not as good as expected.

6. Sam became crazy, _____ with excitement about money and silver.

7. Brigham Young _____ that having many wives was too much trouble.

8. His dreams of getting rich _____ when he saw how hard mining was.

3. Make Inferences

To make an inference, we combine what we see and hear in the story with what we already know—our background knowledge—to make conclusions, or inferences, about a character or situation. In this exercise, more than one answer may be right.

Example: Make an inference about what kind of person went out west.

Here are some possible answers: Most of the men had **ambition** and were adventurous.
Most of the men were single, not family men.

1. **A Stagecoach Trip:** Make an inference about what Mark Twain thought about Brigham Young.
2. **The Terrible Desert:** Make an inference about why Twain sneaked around, hid, and didn't want anyone to see him looking for silver or gold.
3. **Gold and Silver Everywhere!:** Make an inference about why Twain didn't tell his partners about his treasures right away.
4. **Fool's Gold:** Make an inference about why Twain took the reporter's job.
5. Make an inference about why he chose the pen name of Mark Twain.

4. Talk About It

Discuss these questions with a partner or in a small group:
1. Why didn't Sam like to fight in the Civil War?
2. What were the difficulties of a long stagecoach trip in the 1860s?
3. Do you know of other times that men rushed somewhere to get rich fast?
4. Would you rush somewhere for gold? Do you buy lottery tickets? Is it the same?
5. In the **Fool's Gold** section, what did Sam mean when he said, "My lesson was that I treat men this way too, **underrating** men of gold and glorifying men of **mica.**"?

5. Write What You Think

1. Write a letter by Sam's brother about the Nevada **territory.**
2. Write a diary entry for a day on the stagecoach.
3. Write about any of the discussion questions above.
4. Write a description of one of Mark Twain's **adventures.**

6. Play the Part

Choose a situation below. Plan a dialogue between the characters and act it out.
1. **Sam and his mother.** She doesn't want him to go west; he tells her why he's going.
2. **Brigham Young and Sam.** Young wants Sam to marry his daughter. Sam wants to leave.
3. **Sam and the stagecoach driver.** Sam wants to drive the coach; the driver says no.
4. **Sam, Mr. Ballou, and another miner.** They argue about the value of what Sam found.
5. **Sam and Orion.** Sam wants to go to Virginia City; Orion asks him to stay in Carson City.
6. **Sam and the owner of the *Enterprise*.** Sam wants more money to work as a reporter.

7. Story Theater

1. Work with a group of students.
2. Choose a section of the story with the class.
3. Read the section with your group. With your group decide which role you will play. If possible, change everything to conversation. Feel free to change the description to conversation. Choose any props you wish.
4. Practice your section for 15–20 minutes with your group.
5. Perform your story for the class. Try to make the story theater flow from one part to the next.

Johnny Comes Marching Home Again

Words to Understand

Read the sentences. Discuss what the words in **boldface** mean.

Words About the Economy

1. The northern economy was **industrial,** with factories, but the southern was **agricultural,** more dependent on farming.
2. Many southern farms were huge; they were called **plantations,** and they usually grew one **crop,** such as cotton or tobacco.
3. Plantation owners needed many workers, and they liked having **slave** labor.

Words About Wars and Armies

1. During a war, the **heroes** may find **glory,** but they also get **blisters** on their feet.
2. A **civil** war is fought between two groups in the same country.
3. When a war is over, one side **surrenders**, or gives up.
4. The boys have **nightmares** about the terrible things, the **horror and misery** of war.
5. The side that wins is **victorious,** claims a **victory.**

Words About Emotions and People

1. She **chased** the pig that was **wild** from the noise of the bells and cannon.
2. We **celebrate** birthdays and holidays with food and parties.
3. Johnny had **pride** about doing a good job as a soldier.
4. People can be **weak** from many things, even from emotion.
5. **"Goodness gracious"** is an expression of surprise.

Active Vocabulary Learning Activity

Work in pairs on a word or phrase your teacher gives you. Try to show or illustrate it. For example, if your phrase is "shoot arrows," you can say the phrase and at the same time make the physical motion of "shooting an arrow." If you wish, you can also make some gesture or facial expression related to the vocabulary.

Finally, repeat the word or the phrase and action with the class. Here are the words to use in this story:

> surrender, celebrate, tossed, cannon, slave, blisters, wild, nightmare, horror and misery, weak, board.

*I*n the mid-19th century, differences between the northern and southern states caused a bloody war. The war had several causes. One was slavery. Another cause was the **agricultural** South's fear of being controlled by the **industrial** North. Rich southerners depended on slaves for their large **plantation** economy. Southerners wanted slavery to spread to new states, to keep a balance. When they feared losing the balance, the southern states voted to leave the union and form a new nation, the Confederate States of America. As president, Abraham Lincoln fought to keep the country united. After four hard years this Civil War, or War Between the States, ended in 1865. General Robert E. Lee, the commander of the Confederate Army **surrendered** to General Ulysses S. Grant, the leader of the Union Forces. This story is about one soldier's return home.

Johnny Comes Marching Home Again

Out of the Army

"Hey, Johnny, now that the war is over, are you headed home to your sweetheart?" asked Jeff.

"She's not my girl anymore. She married my older brother."

Jeff was surprised, but he said, "Don't worry about that. There are girls
5 everywhere. See that girl over there. She's looking at you in your uniform.
I think she likes you."

Johnny smiled at the girl as he passed.

All along the road, people were cheering the **victorious** soldiers, "Hurrah, Hurrah."

10 "Why don't you come out west with me?" Jeff asked.

"I never thought of that. For three years I planned to return home as a hero and marry Susanna. I loved her so much."

"I've been thinking about going west. It's new and open. I'm going to St. Louis and maybe all the way to California. Come with me," said Jeff.

15 "Maybe so. First, come with me to my family's farm near Cincinnati," said Johnny.

That night Johnny and Jeff lay around the campfire. Their last night in the army, the boys talked about their three years together.

"We were so young when we joined up." said Jeff.

20 "Yeah. When I left Cincinnati, I was 15," said Johnny. "I expected war to be fun and full of **glory.** Instead, it was marching, marching, marching. Worn-out boots. **Blisters.** Cold, damp tents. Then mud, bad meat, hard biscuits, freezing nights, and wet, smelly blankets. Not a lot of fun."

Union and Confederate soldiers fought bitterly at Gettysburg.

Fun Turned into Nightmares

"At first it was fun," said Jeff. "Marching to the pipes and the drums, being
in parades. It was great until Gettysburg. Ten of my buddies died in that
battle. I'll have **nightmares** about that until I die."

"I have **nightmares** too. My worst ones are in the field hospital there, and
seeing doctors cut off all those arms and legs, a whole wagon full. So much
horror and **misery.**"

"I forgot about that, and half of them died anyway." Jeff shook his head,
as if to shake the memory out. "We'd better go to sleep."

Johnny couldn't sleep. He started thinking about Susanna and his brother.
How could Robert do that? How could he take my girl away? He couldn't
march with his bad knee so he stayed home on the farm. Her letter said,
"Johnny, I hope this doesn't disappoint you, but I'm marrying Robert. You
never asked me to marry you. We weren't engaged." And then she added,
"I'll always love you like a brother."

The next day they lined up for their last pay: $13 a month and an extra
$5 for victory. New printed money. They shouldered their bags and walked
west toward the Ohio River.

The riverboat trip to Cincinnati was fun. Everyone treated them like
heroes. Two young ladies shared their food with them. It was like a holiday.
Johnny forgot about Susanna.

But when he got off the boat, there she was. "Look, Jeff, there's Susanna.
45 What's she doing here? She looks the same."

Johnny walked over to her. "Well, I didn't expect to see you right away.
That letter of yours hurt me badly. Why didn't you wait for me?" His voice was
full of emotion. Standing next to her made him **weak.**

"Have you forgotten me?"

"I beg your pardon. Do I know you?" asked the young girl, sur-
50 prised by the handsome young man in uniform.

"Susanna. Have you forgotten me so fast?"

"Susanna?" she asked, still surprised that this handsome soldier
was talking to her.

"Susanna, I thought you were going to marry ME."

55 "**Goodness gracious.** I'm not Susanna. I'm her younger sister,
Rosie."

Johnny remembered "little Rosie" as a child. She'd changed
so much in three years. She looked like his picture of Susanna.

"You're Johnny! Susanna and Robert live in Indiana now."
60 Rosie said. "You're a hero. Did you fight at Gettysburg?" That
was the start of their friendship.

A week later the whole town **celebrated** the end of the war
with a parade and picnic. Johnny and Jeff marched in the parade.
Along the street, the crowd cheered "Hurrah, hurrah." Little girls
65 **tossed** roses on the street as the soldiers passed.

Marching in front of the village hall, the boys felt the same
pride they'd felt when they joined the army. They knew it was
a good cause. It was important to save the union and to free
the **slaves.**

70 When they marched by the village hall, the bells rang, then a cannon was
fired. The **mayor** rose to speak. Everyone was quiet. Then suddenly there was a
loud noise. A girl ran through the parade, **chasing** a runaway pig. It was Rosie.

The pig crashed into the chairs. She headed for the mayor. Johnny ran to
stop the pig, but she hit the mayor, and he fell on top of the pig. Then the pig
75 jumped up and ran toward the picnic tables in the churchyard.

After the Pig

Rosie and Johnny both caught up with her. They crashed and tumbled on
top of the pig. "Meet Flora, my **prize** pig. The cannon drove her **wild."** They
both laughed. They tied Flora to a fence and walked to the picnic tables.
They were first in line for food.
80 The town ladies had brought the food: boiled and roasted corn, roast pig,
roast duck, chicken, fresh pickles, potato salad, and green beans. The desserts
were on another table: peach pudding, lemon meringue pies, apple pies. Jeff
and Johnny hadn't seen food like this since they joined the army.

Here's a popular song from the 1860s

When Johnny Comes Marching Home Again

—WORDS AND MUSIC BY *Patrick S. Gilmore, using the pen name Louis Lambert*

When Johnny comes marching home again,
  Hurrah! Hurrah!
We'll give him a hearty welcome then,
  Hurrah! Hurrah!
The men will cheer, the boys will shout
The ladies they will all turn out
And we'll all feel gay when Johnny comes
  marching home.

The old Church bell will peal with joy,
  Hurrah! Hurrah!
To welcome home our darling boy,
  Hurrah! Hurrah!
The village lads and lassies say
With roses they will strew the way
And we'll all feel gay when Johnny comes
  marching home.

95   They ate near the river. "Johnny, can we leave tomorrow?" asked Jeff.

    "Where are you boys going?" They told Rosie about the plans; then she said, "I want to go."

    "Could you leave your family?" Johnny asked. The three of them found Rosie's mother to ask her **permission.**

100   "No. Rosie, you can't leave home until you're married," said Rosie's mother.

    "Oh, Ma, I'm old enough to take care of myself, and I'll be with Johnny and Jeff."

    "Rosie. You can't. It's not right for a woman to go off alone."

    "Ma'am, I'll marry her," Johnny said.

105   "What? That's crazy. You don't know her," said the older woman.

    "Ma'am, I feel like I've known her forever."

    "Johnny, don't you think you should ask me?"

    "Rosie, will you marry me?" Johnny asked.

    "Oh, Johnny," said Rosie. "I don't want you to marry me just to be nice."

110   "No, Rosie, it's not just to help you. I love you. You're wonderful," he said.

    After the wedding, they **boarded** a riverboat going down the Ohio River toward the Mississippi River: Rosie and Johnny, Jeff, and Flora the pig.

Importance

 The war changed many people's lives. After some young men had lived away from home in other places, they were eager to look for adventure in the open spaces out west. Thus, in its own way, the Civil War contributed to the settling of the west.

Focus on the Story

1. Understand the Story

When did this happen? Put the story events in order by placing the correct number 1–7 in the blank. The first event in the story is chosen for you.

_____   Flora the pig messes up the parade.

___1___   Johnny and Jeff join the Army.

_____   Johnny, Rosie, Jeff, and Flora leave for the West.

_____   The war ends in 1865.

_____   They fight at the Battle of Gettysburg in 1863.

_____   Johnny meets Rosie.

_____   Johnny asks Rosie to marry him.

2. Practice Vocabulary

Use these words to complete the sentences:

proud   prize   nightmares   glory
tossed   mayor   permission   board

1. After the battle of Gettysburg, he had _____ about it for years.

2. When people fight in wars, they sometimes find fame and _____.

3. The children gently _____ the flowers in the road.

4. When you get on something, like a boat or a train, you _____ it.

5. Johnny felt _____ because he had helped save the union and free the slaves.

6. The pig Flora won a _____ for being the best pig in town.

7. The elected leader of the town is called the _____.

8. Children need _____ from their parents to do things.

3. Understand the Characters' Problems

Read about Susanna's problem and her solution; then fill in the missing problems or solutions for the other characters.

CHARACTER	PROBLEM	SOLUTION
Susanna	1. Wants to marry Robert	1. She writes Johnny a letter.
Johnny	2. Wants Rosie to go west with them	2. _____
Rosie	3. Her pig runs through the parade	3. _____
	4. _____	4. Tells Johnny "Don't marry me just to be nice."
Jeff	5. Doesn't want to go west alone	5. _____

4. Talk About It

Discuss these questions with a partner or in a small group:
1. Was it wrong or disloyal for Susanna to marry Robert?
2. Was Susanna Johnny's sweetheart? Or was it his dream?
3. What would you do if you owned slaves?
4. Do you know of other countries that had slavery? When?
5. What if the south had won the war? How would things be different?

5. Write What You Think

1. Write a letter from Johnny to Susanna, either before or after he received the news about her marriage to Robert.
2. Write a short newspaper account about the end of the war.
3. Write an entry for a day in the journal of a soldier in the Civil War.
4. Write a paper about why slavery is wrong.

6. Play the Part

Choose a situation below. Plan a dialogue between the characters and act it out.
1. **Johnny, Jeff.** Johnny wants Jeff to come to his farm; Jeff wants Johnny to go west with him.
2. **Robert, Susanna.** Robert wants to get married; Susanna says, "What about Johnny?"
3. **Johnny, Rosie, her mother.** Johnny says he wants to marry Rosie; the mother says no; what does Rosie say?
4. **Johnny, his father.** Johnny wants to go out west. His father wants him to stay at home.

7. Geography Focus

On the map below find the places mentioned in the questions. Write the answers.
1. Where did Johnny and Jeff start their trip?
2. Where is Ohio in relation to Washington, D.C.?
3. Which city is farther west, St. Louis or Cincinnati?
4. Which is farther east, Gettysburg or New York City?
5. On the map, trace the routes of the two riverboats—down the _____ River to Cincinnati, and then later to the _____ River.
6. Which river would they have to travel on to get to Kansas City?

Chapter 7

1867: The Chinese Strike Against the Railroad

BEFORE YOU READ

Answer the following questions.

1. Have you ever ridden on a train? Where? Compare train travel to stagecoach travel in the Mark Twain story.

2. How hard is it to build a railroad?

3. What is a **strike**? Do workers have a right to strike?

Words to Understand

Read the sentences. Discuss what the words in **boldface** mean.

Words About Work

1. The workers wanted more money. They decided to **strike,** to stop working.
2. Workers join together and form **unions.**
3. He was **skilled** in using dynamite, but was **still** not paid more.
4. The boss **hired** the Chinese.

Words About Building the Railroad

1. **Dynamite** is an explosive.
2. The workers had to **lay track** for the train.
3. In the mountains the train goes through **tunnels.**
4. The tools were **shovels** and **hammers.**
5. **Nitroglycerine** is a dynamite that makes bigger explosions, bigger **blasts.**
6. The sound of dynamite **echoed** in the valley.

Words About People and Actions

1. The Chinese **quit** work, decided to go on strike.
2. The boss **locked away** (made unavailable) the food.
3. Sometimes one group of people is **prejudiced** against (dislikes without reason) another group.
4. One man **warned** another not to go back.
5. Yee Chen said that they **treated** the Chinese really badly, like slaves.
6. Building railroad tracks in the mountains is really **difficult.**

Active Vocabulary Learning Activity

Work in pairs on a word or phrase your teacher gives you. Try to show or illustrate it. For example, if your phrase is "shoot arrows," you can say the phrase and at the same time make the physical motion of "shooting an arrow." If you wish, you can also make some gesture or facial expression related to the vocabulary.

Finally, repeat the word or the phrase and action with the class. Here are the words to use in this story:

blasts, shovels, hammers, echoed, hired, lay the track, starve, tunnel, warned, locked away.

*E*veryone wanted a railroad across America. The Union Pacific (U.P.) built the railroad west from Nebraska. The Central Pacific (C.P.) built east from California. The U.P. **hired** Irish men in Boston and New York, but the C.P. couldn't find enough workers in California. The work on the railroad was very **difficult.** From Sacramento the railroad would rise 10,000 feet in the mountains in just 100 miles. Most workers stayed only long enough to make money to go mining. Then they left. After two years only 56 miles of **track had been laid.** Then Charles Crocker, the C.P. track boss, hired Chinese laborers. The Chinese men worked hard, but they weren't paid as much as other men were. This story is about the Chinese strike against the railroad in June 1867. It is told by Ah Chu, the head man (leader) of the Chinese workers.

1867: The Chinese Strike Against the Railroad

Dynamite is Dangerous

"Ah Chu, tell Big Boss we won't work anymore," said one angry worker.

"We won't **dynamite.** We won't lay the tracks. No work unless they give us what we want," said Wing Ho, the leader of the younger workers.

I spoke up. "Well, what do you want?"

5   Wing Ho said, "We want the same pay as the white workers. We don't want to work with this new dynamite. We want shorter hours. We want to be free to look for other jobs."

"Yes, they **treat** us like slaves," added Yee Chen, another young worker. "Boss man walks up and down with a big stick in his hand and a cigar in his 10 mouth, saying we can't leave here. Also we want to work like the white man, only eight hours a day."

It is difficult being the head man. My group chose me to be their leader, to count their hours, to collect their pay, and to buy food.

They chose me because I know a little English. The boss tells me what to 15 do. Then I tell the men. My job is hard. I'm between my people and the boss, and I don't like that.

Wing Ho joined Ah Chu in his tent to eat their evening rice. "Ah Chu, our group wants to **strike.** All our people want to **strike.** We are angry. We do the hard work. We want more money. Some want to leave this job for another. 20 Big Boss treats us like slaves."

"I understand. The work is dangerous, and I want it to be safer. Ten of our men were killed last week with that new dynamite. It's bad." I agreed with Wing. "But I'm not the boss. I want you men to be safe, but you know I must please the boss too. They pay us. We must give them good work."

The Chinese Ask for More

25 "But, Ah Chu, you know we work hard. They can't make us work more hours. They must give us as much money as the whites." Wing Ho left.

Wing Ho is young. He forgets we get a lot more pay than before. Our families in China want us here. They need the money we send home. My wife and son in China need my money to live. If I didn't work, they would starve.

30 Later that evening, Wing Ho spoke to the workers. "This work is so hard, cutting through the rock with hand **shovels** and **hammers.** Many white men **quit** because it's too hard."

"Many of us know how to use dynamite now, but we **still** get only $1 a day, while the **skilled** white men get $3 to $5 a day," said his friend Yee Chen.

35 "The worst part is the new dynamite, the **nitroglycerine.** That's what happened in Tunnel 5. The first worker hit some **nitroglycerine,** and he was blown up with all his fellows too," added Wing Ho.

I remembered how my brother Po was killed in Tunnel 5, called Red Spur. I went to Boss Strobridge and told him we didn't like the new dynamite. He 40 became angry. "Joe, you can't tell us how to build a railroad." (The whites call me China Joe, but I am really Lee Ah Chu.)

Strobridge talked to Big Boss Crocker that evening. "Isn't that something? Those Chinese think they can tell <u>us</u> how to build a railroad."

Crocker said, "They're good workers, but regular dynamite gives us only 45 seven inches a day. The **nitroglycerine** is dangerous, but it **blasts** the rock. We must use it."

SOURCE: Brown Brothers

Nitroglycerine Kills

The next day they continued using the nitro. China Joe's crew was blasting at the edge of Tunnel 6. Wing Ho set the nitro, and they all ran. The blasts **echoed** through the canyons—one, two, three booms. They waited five 50 minutes, then five more, for another explosion. Then Boss Strobridge yelled, "Go in there now. Back to work. We can't wait all day."

Wing Ho said to China Joe in Chinese, "We must wait longer. There's more nitro in there." All of China Joe's crew heard Wing Ho's **warning** and waited.

55 Boss Strobridge, puffing his cigar, grabbed some other men and pushed them toward the blasting spot. "Get to work. Hurry. Hurry. Hurry. You're slow today."

A young man with his wide straw hat and loose Chinese clothes and heavy American boots walked into the mouth of the **tunnel** and raised his 60 hammer high. As it hit the rock, another loud explosion went off. The young worker died with the flash of the explosion. Eight men around him were killed instantly.

"Oh, I've been hit," yelled Strobridge as he fell to the ground. A piece of flying rock hit his face and he lost one eye.

65 That's when Crocker decided to stop using the nitroglycerine.

That night, June 24, 1867, Lee Ah Chu and his men went to talk to Crocker.

Leland Stanford, one of the railroad builders: "Without the Chinese workers it would be impossible to complete the western portion of this great national highway within the time required by the acts of Congress."

Crocker came to the door. "Sir, the men are unhappy," Ah Chu said. "What do they want?" asked Crocker.

70   "They want $40 a month, as much as the white men are paid. They want the right to leave and get other jobs. They want eight-hour days. They want safer work."

The Workers Strike

Crocker pulled himself up, ready to give a speech. He thought he could always get men to do what he wanted. "Men, we're building a railroad. You must do

50 what you agreed to do. You can't get soft on me. There will be one change. We won't use the nitro anymore." Crocker closed the door.

    The next morning Wing Ho and hundreds of other Chinese **quit** working. They went on **strike.** They refused to work unless they were given more money and more freedom.

55   Strobridge, with a bandage over one eye, walked up and down, yelling at the men, waving his big stick at them. The white workers kept working. They did not join the strike.

    The Chinese sat down. Some played music. Some went hunting and fishing.

    Crocker ordered the food supplies **locked away.** No more work? Then the

60 company would not give them food or water. Most of the Chinese had some food in their tents. They could last a few days.

The Chinese had a harder time than other immigrants. They met more **prejudice.** They differed from most European workers. They wanted to support families at home, not to make new lives here. Charles Crocker, the railroad builder, was happy with the Chinese work force. He refused to use the recently-developed steam drill. Crocker preferred to use the Chinese workers, no matter what the cost to the workers, because the laborers were cheaper.

Chinese workers did not feel welcome at the Promontory Point celebration in 1869.

SOURCE: Culver Pictures

After six days Crocker met with the strikers. "Well, men, I'll give you a choice. Tomorrow is the **deadline.** If you go to work tomorrow, there will be no punishment; but if you don't work tomorrow, you will have to pay the cost
65 of this strike. Also, if you don't go to work, the railroad will give you no more food or water."

The head men translated for the men. The head men met with Crocker and repeated "Eight hours a day good for white man. All the same good for China man." In the end, they reached an agreement.
70 Conditions improved a little for the Chinese workers. At least Crocker was forced to consider the men. The Chinese workers had stood up for their rights.

Importance

Of the 15,000 men who built the railroad east from Sacramento, nine out of ten were Chinese. The Chinese proved how hard they could work. The east and west tracks met in Promontory, Utah, in 1869. The construction of the transcontinental railroad was the outstanding engineering feat of the century. Before 1869 it took months to travel across the country. With the railroad it took less than a week.

Focus on the Story

1. Understand the Story

Circle the letter of the best answer.
1. Most Chinese came to America because they wanted
   a. to build the railroad.
   b. to make money to send back home.
   c. to go to college here.
2. Crocker and Strobridge, the men building the railroad,
   a. paid the Chinese laborers less than they paid white laborers.
   b. wanted to kill the Chinese workers.
   c. were happy to give the Chinese what they wanted.
3. Wing Ho, the young leader,
   a. was lazy and didn't want to work.
   b. wanted to replace Ah Chu as boss.
   c. wanted more pay and better working conditions for his fellow workers.

2. Practice Vocabulary

Use these words to complete the sentences:

blasting   strike   still   lay track
deadline   echoed   prejudiced   warned

1. Big Boss Crocker gave the workers a _____ to go back to work.

2. Some Chinese workers were skilled, but they _____ were paid less than whites.

3. The Chinese workers decided to _____ because they weren't paid as much as the white workers.

4. Many Europeans were _____ against the Chinese.

5. The nitro had much more _____ power than regular dynamite.

6. It was most difficult to _____ in the mountains.

7. The sound of the blasts _____ through the mountains.

8. Wing Ho _____ the men not to go back into the tunnel.

3. Understand Details

Find the incorrect word in each sentence. Cross it out and write the correct word(s) at the end of the sentence.
1. The Chinese were using electric tools to cut the tunnels in the mountains.
2. Wing Ho was demanding more vacation.
3. Nitroglycerine is a safe type of dynamite.
4. The explosion hurt boss man Strobridge's nose.
5. This company was building the railroad westward from California to Utah.
6. The Chinese got paid a lot more in China.
7. Wing Ho wanted the men to work.
8. Boss Crocker buried the nitro because the men got hurt.

4. Talk About It

Discuss these questions with a partner or in a small group:
1. Why was there prejudice between the Chinese and the Europeans?
2. Is there any way to get rid of prejudice?
3. Why did immigrants come to America?
4. Can you guess why Crocker and Strobridge wanted to build the railroad?
5. Is it fair to get laborers to work for a low wage? What would you do if you were boss?

5. Write What You Think

1. Write a letter from Ah Chu to his wife or from Wing Ho to his mother.
2. You are a reporter for a newspaper. Write about Crocker's problem with the workers.
3. Write in detail about the life of one of the Chinese men ten years later.

6. Play the Part

Choose a situation below. Plan a dialogue between the characters and act it out.
1. **Wing Ho, Ah Chu.** Wing Ho wants to strike now. Ah Chu wants the men to wait.
2. **Ah Chu, boss man Strobridge.** Ah Chu states the demands of the men. Strobridge says no.
3. **Wing Ho, Crocker.** Wing Ho tells Crocker the men will strike. Crocker says no.
4. **Boss Strobridge, Crocker.** Strobridge wants to give the workers more money. Crocker wants to pay less so the profits will be bigger.
5. **Reporter, Ah Chu, Strobridge, Wing Ho.** The reporter asks each man about the strike.
6. **Wing Ho, Ah Chu.** After this railroad is complete, Ah Chu wants to go home; Wing Ho wants him to mine for gold.

7. Silent Dialogue Through Writing

Draw a line down the middle of a piece of paper. With a partner, write a dialogue, silently. For example, one person writes something that Wing Ho would say, and passes the paper to his or her partner. The partner writes what Ah Chu might respond.

Chapter 8

The Arrest of
Susan B. Anthony

BEFORE YOU READ

Answer the following questions.

1. **What is your family's attitude toward women's rights?**

2. **Do you feel the same way? How? Why?**

3. **Are equal rights for women important to you? Which rights?**

Words to Understand

Read the sentences. Discuss what the words in **boldface** mean.

Words about Courts and the Legal System

1. The policeman came to **arrest** her, take her to the court.
2. The judge **set the bail at** (said she had to pay) $500.
3. Susan B. demanded **immediate release** (to be let go right now).
4. The judge **denied,** said no to, her requests.
5. The judge did not allow the jury to decide the **verdict** (make the decision).
6. She could not speak **on her own behalf,** for herself.

Government Words

1. The **conservative** view is usually one that doesn't like change.
2. Susan B. felt it was her **duty,** her obligation, to vote.
3. The **election inspectors** could decide to let someone vote or not.
4. Susan B. tested her **constitutional right** to vote, whether it was correct according to the Constitution.
5. Susan B. said women would get the vote through an **amendment** to the Constitution.

Emotional Verbs

1. The women wanted to **challenge,** to resist or oppose, the law that said they couldn't vote.
2. She **embarrassed,** distressed, the young man in public.
3. She wouldn't go willingly; he had to **force** her to go.
4. He felt guilty for arresting her and wanted to **apologize** for it.
5. Men **ridiculed** (made fun of) women's wanting to vote.

Active Vocabulary Learning Activity

Work in pairs on a word or phrase your teacher gives you. Try to show or illustrate it. For example, if your phrase is "shoot arrows," you can say the phrase and at the same time make the physical motion of "shooting an arrow." If you wish, you can also make some gesture or facial expression related to the vocabulary.

Finally, repeat the word or the phrase and action with the class.
Here are the words to use in this story:

embarrass, force, denied, challenge, ridicule, apologize, arrest, opponent.

*S*tarting in 1848, some American women demanded the right to vote. Strangely enough, as American politics became more democratic in the 1800s, the attitude toward women had become more **conservative.** Earlier, women had the vote in some states, but in the 1820s, state legislatures took that right from women. Elizabeth Cady Stanton and Susan B. Anthony led the cause to get the vote for women. In 1872, after fighting for the vote for 20 years, Susan B. (as she was called) wanted to test the Constitution's position on women voting. She forced the **election inspectors** in her city to allow her to vote. She was convinced that, as a citizen, she had a **constitutional right** to vote, and felt that it was her **duty** to go to court to test this right. She convinced other women to do the same. Ms. Anthony tells her own story here.

The Arrest of Susan B. Anthony

"You're under arrest!"

When I answered the door on November 18, 1872, I was surprised to see a young policeman standing there. "What can I do for you, young man?"

"I am sorry, Miss Anthony, but I have come to **arrest** you." He handed me
5 papers that said I had voted, knowing I did not have the lawful right to vote.

"I am a citizen, and I have a right to vote," I said.

"Sorry, Madam, this says you are guilty of a crime. If you are convicted, you could be fined up to $500 or be put in prison for three years." The young man almost **apologized** for what he was doing.

10 "It was not a crime because as a citizen I have a duty to vote."

"Madam, I don't have to bring you in. It would be all right if you just went to see the judge by yourself tomorrow."

"Oh, no, young man, I will not go unless you **force** me to go." I wanted to make this important.

15 "I guess I'll have to take you in, then," he said.

When we got on the streetcar and the driver wanted my fare, I **embarrassed** the policeman more by saying, "This gentleman is taking me to jail. Ask him for the money." I was not making it easy for him.

I wanted to test the law. Surely women did have the right to vote.

20 "Yes, I voted," I said proudly to the judge, "I believe women have the right to vote. Even though the Constitution doesn't say we have the right to vote, it doesn't say that we don't."

The Judge Sets the Bail

"All the women voters and the election inspectors who let them vote are accused of a crime. I **set the bail at** $500 each," said the judge.

25 "I refuse to pay bail," I said. "and I demand **immediate release** and I **challenge** the lawfulness of my arrest," I said.

Women of all ages marched for the right to vote.

"**Denied,**" said the judge, "and I increase your bail to $1,000."

"I refuse to give bail money; I prefer jail," I said. Personally I wanted to challenge this all the way to the Supreme Court.

30 However, my lawyer did not want to see me in jail, and he paid my bail. This prevented me from taking the case to the Supreme Court.

In the months before the trial, I gave talks almost every night—in Ohio, Indiana, Illinois. My speeches about the "equal right of all citizens to the vote" were convincing.

35 I quoted the Constitution, "It was we, the people—not we, the white male citizens, but we the whole people—who formed this Union. And we formed it to make the blessings of liberty safe, not for the half of ourselves and the half of our children but for the whole people—women as well as men."

One of my speeches was titled "State Laws Relating to Married Women 40 Have Placed Them in the Position of Slaves." I spoke every night for three weeks in all the towns around the city where my trial was to be. I wanted women to know what was happening.

The press reported, "The majority of these law-breakers are elderly, mature-looking women with thoughtful faces, just the sort I would like to see in charge 45 of my sick-room, considerate, patient, kindly."

Susan B. is Ridiculed

My campaign received nationwide publicity, but much of the press **ridiculed** me as a **homely** woman. It was hard to be ridiculed, but in my hometown of Rochester, New York, I was respected and beloved. My hometown paper praised me "for my common sense and loyalty."

Elizabeth Cady Stanton and I had been fighting for this right to vote ever since she made the demand for the vote at the First Women's Conference held in Seneca Falls, New York, in 1848. Stanton's request for the vote for women was called **ridiculous** and comical. Women's rights were a joke to men.

My trial started on June 17, 1873. My sister Hannah was with me, and so were my two lawyers. I faced an all-male jury.

"Hannah, how can they understand how I feel after being arrested and ridiculed for voting?"

"Yes, Susan, you were arrested for exercising the rights of a citizen."

But Judge Ward Hunt was not a fair man. He was an **opponent** of women's rights. "The accused may not speak **on her own behalf,**" the judge ruled. Thus I was silenced.

But my lawyer was convincing in his arguments. "If the same act had been done by her brother under the same circumstances, the act would have been innocent and honorable; but having been done by a woman, it is said to be a crime . . . I believe this is the first time that a woman has been tried in a criminal court, merely on account of her sex."

Without even giving the case to the jury, Judge Hunt took out a paper and read, "The right of voting is a right given to us by the state, not the United States. Therefore, there is no question for the jury and I direct the jury to find a **verdict** of guilty."

Failure is Impossible

Judge Hunt refused to let the jury decide.

The judge then asked, "Has the prisoner anything to say?"

I had a lot to say. "Yes, your honor," and I told him "You have stepped on all my rights. Your denial of my citizen's right to vote is the denial of my right of consent as one of the governed . . ."

"The Court orders the prisoner to sit down," shouted Judge Hunt. "It will not allow another word."

After this, I knew that justice for women could not be found in the courts. I realized we had to work again for an **amendment** to the Constitution.

It is hard. Everywhere I see that the whiskey makers, drinkers, gamblers are against us, and then at the other extreme the selfish religious conservatives hate us also. When I get discouraged, I must remember that when we started this fight, in the early 1850s, women could not even speak out in public, so we have made progress.

Anthony and Stanton worked for the cause in state after state, as the women's right to vote was introduced. But when Susan B. died in 1906, women had the vote in only four states, all western states: Wyoming, Colorado, Utah, and Idaho. Eleven other states gave women the vote by the time the **amendment** was passed in 1920.

In Susan B's last public speech, at her 86th birthday celebration, she urged the next generation to continue the work, declaring, "Failure is impossible."

Importance

Why did women work so long without success? What force had the power to stand up against their gentle persistent persuasion? It was the alcohol lobby. People who made money on alcohol spread the rumor that if women were able to vote, they would pass a law prohibiting all alcohol. The alcohol lobby repeated this rumor in state after state, and was usually successful in defeating women's vote. Stanton and Anthony worked for the cause for more than 50 years, but neither one lived long enough to see the 19th amendment to the Constitution that gave the right to vote to women in 1920. This amendment was passed two years after men voted in the 18th **amendment,** the prohibition amendment that made alcohol illegal. The 18th **amendment** eliminated the alcohol force that had kept women from getting the vote all those years.

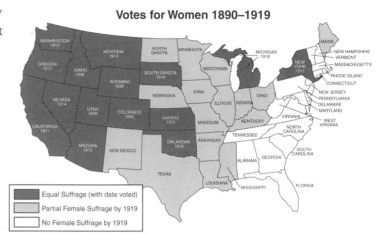

Votes for Women 1890–1919

- Equal Suffrage (with date voted)
- Partial Female Suffrage by 1919
- No Female Suffrage by 1919

Focus on the Story

I. Understand the Story

Find out. Read the question. Find the answer in the story. Write it on the line.

> **Example:** Why was Susan B. Anthony arrested?
> <u>Because she had voted, and she was female.</u>

1. Who were the two most important women in the fight for women to vote?

   _____

2. Why did Susan B. vote in the 1872 election? _____

   _____

3. What in the Constitution led Susan B. to think she had the right to vote?

   _____

4. What bail did the judge set for Susan B.? _____

   _____

5. How was Susan B. described by the press? _____

   _____

6. Which states were first to give women the right to vote? _____

   _____

2. Practice Vocabulary

Use these words to complete the sentences.

| challenge | opponent | homely | apologized |
| denied | duty | embarrass | conservative |

1. He _____ because he felt bad about arresting her.

2. The _____ people were against women voting.

3. The judge was an _____ of women's rights.

4. He was very uncomfortable, _____ to arrest her.

5. Susan B. wanted to _____ the law.

6. Because she was not beautiful, many called her _____.

7. The judge _____ her rights.

8. Susan B. thought it was her _____ as a citizen to vote.

3. Understand Details

Find the incorrect word in each sentence. Cross it out and write the correct word(s) at the end of the sentence.
1. The judge said she could speak on her own behalf.
2. The policeman arrested Elizabeth Cady Stanton.
3. Susan B. agreed to give bail money.
4. The press said that Susan B. was beautiful.
5. Most men wanted women to get the vote.
6. Susan B. said, "Judge Hunt is a fair man."
7. Susan B. lived long enough to see women vote in the United States.
8. It was the church lobby (interest) that stopped women from getting the vote.

4. Talk About It

Discuss these questions with a partner or in a small group:
1. "Two heads are better than one" is an English proverb. Stanton and Anthony worked together. Why would this proverb be true for this cause?
2. What are the similarities and differences between the situation of women in your native country today and that of the American women in 1872; economic, social, political?
3. Is there still discrimination against women in the world, economically, socially, or politically?
4. Are all jobs and professions open to both men and women in the countries you know?
5. What kind of child care would you suggest for the many young mothers who work?

5. Write What You Think

1. Choose any question from Section 4. Write a one-page answer.
2. Write a newspaper article about Susan B. Anthony.
3. Write a comparison of women's rights then and now, in any country.

6. Play the Part

Choose one of the situations below. Plan a dialogue between the characters and act it out.
1. **Susan B, policeman.** She wants to embarrass him. He wants her to go by herself.
2. **Susan B, her lawyer.** She wants to go to jail; he wants to give her bail money.
3. **Susan B, Judge Hunt.** She says he is wrong in many ways; he accuses her of crime.
4. **Susan B, Mrs. Stanton.** They disagree about Susan B. voting, or something else about getting women's rights.
5. **Susan B, a reporter.** He says her work for the vote is ridiculous; she tells him why it is important.
6. **Women, alcohol lobbyist.** They argue about why women shouldn't get the vote.

7. Silent Dialogue Through Writing

Draw a line down the middle of a piece of paper. With a partner, write a dialogue, silently. For example, one person writes something that Susan B. Anthony would say, and passes the paper to his or her partner. The partner writes what Judge Hunt might respond.

Chief Joseph

Answer the following questions.

1. What do you know about the people who lived here before the Europeans came, the **indigenous** peoples of the Americas?

2. Did the **indigenous** people or Native Americans (called Indians by mistake) have **rights** to their lands?

Words to Understand

Read the sentences. Discuss what the words in **boldface** mean.

Words About Native Americans and the Frontier
1. Chief Joseph **belonged to** the Nez Perce **tribe.**
2. The young fighting men in the tribe were called **braves** or **warriors.**
3. **Indigenous** means occurring naturally or living in an area.
4. **Indigenous** Americans usually call their God the **Great Spirit.**
5. A **teepee** was a type of movable home.
6. The telegraph was called the **"singing wire"** by the Nez Perce.
7. A **medicine man** was a priest, a holy man, and a doctor, all in one person.

Words About Fighting
1. The government promised the tribes many things in **treaties,** but did not **keep the promises.**
2. It was a great **injustice** to break the promises made in the treaties.
3. The young braves wanted to **take revenge** on the settlers (to hurt them for the **injustice**).
4. Some braves called Joseph **cowardly** (fearful) because he didn't want to fight.
5. Many European settlers did not believe the tribal people had **rights** to the land.
6. The army chased Chief Joseph's tribe and tried to **block** their **escape route.**

FACTS TO KNOW

*T*he tribe of Chief Joseph, the Nez Perce, was known as noble and peace-loving. In 1805 they welcomed Lewis and Clark, who explored the west for President Thomas Jefferson. Later, when the settlers came, they tried to take the land, the Wallowa Valley, away from this tribe. There were **treaties,** but this group of the Nez Perce refused to sign the treaties. They were called "non-treaty". Most people knew the land legally **belonged to** the Nez Perce. In 1876, one of General Howard's officers reported that Joseph and his group owned all that land by law. But the settlers were coming in. "In 1877, the government ordered the non-treaty Nez Perce to go to the reservation. To their pleadings against this **injustice,** the menacing reply was the gathering of troops to force them." (*New York Times,* Oct. 15, 1877, p. 4).

They were being forced onto a small reservation away from their lands. Because of all this **injustice,** some young Nez Perce reacted and killed some settlers. The war started, and Joseph and his group of 700 Nez Perce tried to run away. This story starts right after the first battle.

Chief Joseph

June 17: A Baby is Born in White Bird Canyon

Alokut walked into Joseph's teepee.

Joseph was looking into the face of his newborn infant, "She chose a moment of victory to come into the world."

"Wind Song, your baby girl is fine. How lucky we are that she waited to
5 come until the battle was over," said Alokut.

"Yes," said Wind Song, Joseph's wife, "The **Great Spirit** smiled on us and gave us victory."

"Father, give me the baby now," said Sarah, Joseph's older daughter.

The two men stepped outside the teepee. Joseph said, "Ah, brother, I can-
10 not believe that we are fighting. We cannot win against the rapid-firing guns and cannon and the **'singing wire.'** I know that it is better to live at peace than to begin a war and lie dead. Many of the young **braves** called me a **coward** because I did not want to fight."

"You are a brave man," said Alokut.

15 "This battle against Captain Perry went well. None of our men died, but Captain Perry lost a third of his men, 34 dead. How many guns did the soldiers leave?"

Alokut reported. "We found 63 rifles and many pistols after they ran away. We are stronger now, and our warriors are happy."

20 "I have always voted against war, but I must save my people now. I cannot control the hot-blooded, hot-headed braves. They want **revenge.** They are ready to die rather than live with the white man's injustice."

"Yes, our braves are ready for more battle, but already General Howard is calling for soldiers to chase us down."

25 "We cannot fight against One-Armed Howard and his big guns. We must outrun them, even with our 400 women, children, and old people."

"But Joseph, where can we go?"

Joseph said, "I do not know. Will he let us go, or will he chase us down? Are we so important? Maybe we can disappear into the **wilderness.**"

30 But already news had reached Washington about the Nez Perce.

July 11–14: No Clear Victory at Clearwater River

"I must leave with the women and children," said Chief Joseph.

Chief Looking Glass agreed. "We have fought for two days; this is enough fighting for now."

"Joseph, go now with the women and children. We will hold General
35 Howard here until you get to the Lolo Pass in the wild Bitterroot Mountains," said White Bird.

Joseph walked to his teepee. "Sarah, take care of Wind Song and little sister. I will be leading," said Joseph and he walked ahead.

A few hours later General Howard could not believe what he saw. "Look!
40 The Indians are across the river. They are getting away."

"How will we follow? We have no boats. With all these heavy guns we can-not chase them." As Howard and his men watched helplessly, the last Nez Perce **slipped** soundlessly into the wilderness of the Bitterroot Mountains.

"What do the **scouts** say?" asked General Howard.

45   "Joseph went ahead with the women, children, old people . . . 400 of them. The other chiefs—Looking Glass, Alokut, the rest of the young men—waited until they were ahead."

"How many horses do they have?" asked Howard.

"Two thousand."

50   "We will chase them down the Lolo Trail, pulling our big guns and camp **equipment.**"

The soldiers waited for boats, crossed the river, and chased them into the mud and rain, up and down the mountains. But the Indians were faster. The soldiers, slowed down by their heavy cannon, could not catch them.

July 25: Nine Days Later at "Fort Fizzle"

55 The Indians came out of the wilderness.

"Joseph, we have left Howard far behind, but there is a fort ahead, and it is **blocking** our route into the Bitteroot valley," said Alokut.

"Looking Glass is meeting with the army captain there, but we don't want to fight. My plan is to go around their fort by climbing the hills and going safely 60 past the soldiers," said Joseph.

"The whites think such an **escape route** is impossible." said Alokut.

Sarah carried her new sister on her back. "Come mother, hold my hand."

"Do not worry, daughter I am strong again," said Joseph's wife.

Once past the soldiers, in the valley, Sarah said, "Mother, I will use some 65 gold to buy flour, coffee, sugar, and tobacco from the settlers."

"Yes," said Wind Song "The settlers see that we keep the peace and we don't want to fight. They will sell food to us."

They went through a settled valley but did nothing **hostile.**

Meanwhile, people all over the country were **cheering for** the Nez Perce 70 in their run for freedom. The chase was being read about on the east coast, and many Americans hoped the brave Nez Perce would get away from the army.

August 8: The Terrible Battle of the Big Hole Camp

"Joseph, we have left Howard far behind," said Alokut.

"We will rest here," said Chief Looking Glass. "We can fish, cut wood, hunt deer."

75   White Bird said, "Let's keep on the trail. We must keep going."

One **medicine man** said "We must hurry through this country. If we stop, there will be tears in our eyes." He was warning them that it was not safe to stay still. But the braves felt safe, and no one stood watch that night. That was a terrible mistake because the soldiers knew where they were.

80   The **"singing wire"** (the telegraph) was telling the army where the Nez Perce were. Colonel Gibbon marched and attacked them in the early morning. It was a surprise attack.

The battle was terrible, with many dying on both sides. Later that day, some young warriors stole Gibbon's cannon. Because they didn't know how to 85 shoot it, they buried it.

On his deathbed in 1871, old Joseph warned his son not to sell his homeland. "When I am gone, think of your land. You are the chief of these people. Always remember that your father never sold the land. You must stop your ears whenever you are asked to sign a treaty selling your home. A few years more, and the white man will be all around you. They have their eyes on this land. My son, never forget my dying words. This country holds your father's body. Never sell the bones of your father and your mother."

The Nez Perce lost many loved ones. Their **mourning** was so loud that Colonel Gibbon wrote, "Few of us will soon forget the wail of mingled grief, rage, and horror which came from the Indian camp 400 yards from us when the Indians recognized their slaughtered warriors, women and children."

90 Again, Joseph left with the women and children, but his wife Wind Song was one of the dead. Alokut's wife died in this battle also. Joseph was surprised that the white men would attack a sleeping village, "The Nez Perce never make war on women and children; we would **be ashamed** to do so."

The white soldiers said, "The Indian women were shooting too."

95 The Nez Perce hurried across southwestern Montana.

"We must follow Sitting Bull into Canada." said Joseph. Sitting Bull was a chief of the Dakota tribe who had fled to Canada the year before.

White Bird agreed. "Yes. These soldiers will chase us forever. We must go where they cannot follow."

September: In the Yellowstone Valley

100 "General Howard is still chasing us, " said Joseph.

"He will be slow now," said Alokut. "I went to his camp during the night and drove away many of his horses."

As they ran away, the Nez Perce crossed the newly created Yellowstone National Park. There they scared some tourists who had come to see the
105 beautiful scenery.

Whenever possible, they would run away from a fight. "Colonel Sturgis set a trap in the upper Yellowstone Valley," said Joseph, "but we went through the wilderness and got to his rear."

In Canyon Creek on September 13, they stole a stagecoach, but the chiefs
110 tried to keep the braves from harming anyone.

Now it was a race for the Canadian **border.** The Indians were **exhausted** by the long flight, but they hurried across the plains to the Bear Paw Mountains. Thirty miles from Canada, they paused to rest, confident that they had gotten away from their pursuers.

115 Once more they were wrong. Because of the **"singing wire,"** this rest ended in their last stand.

October 1–5: Defeat at the Bear Paw Mountains

From Fort Keogh in the east came Colonel Nelson Miles with 600 men racing across Montana. He wanted to catch the Nez Perce before they crossed the border.

120 The soldiers attacked, surprising the Nez Perce in three groups. The soldiers chased the horses away, making escape impossible. About 104 Nez Perce did escape during the five-day battle. They went to Canada; Sarah was among them. Joseph's five-month old baby daughter remained with her father.

The fight lasted five days. The remaining war leaders, including the brave
125 Alokut, were killed. Some braves still wanted to fight, but Joseph pointed to the starving women and children. "For myself I do not care. It is for them I am going to surrender." Joseph surrendered his people to Colonel Miles and General Howard on October 5.

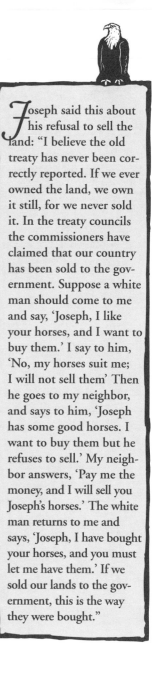

Joseph said this about his refusal to sell the land: "I believe the old treaty has never been correctly reported. If we ever owned the land, we own it still, for we never sold it. In the treaty councils the commissioners have claimed that our country has been sold to the government. Suppose a white man should come to me and say, 'Joseph, I like your horses, and I want to buy them.' I say to him, 'No, my horses suit me; I will not sell them' Then he goes to my neighbor, and says to him, 'Joseph has some good horses. I want to buy them but he refuses to sell.' My neighbor answers, 'Pay me the money, and I will sell you Joseph's horses.' The white man returns to me and says, 'Joseph, I have bought your horses, and you must let me have them.' If we sold our lands to the government, this is the way they were bought."

SOURCE: Department of the Interior, National Park Service, Nez-Perce National PArk #NEPE-HI-0364

Nez Perce chiefs and braves on the reservation after their surrender.

130   After a flight of 120 days and 1,700 miles, and only 30 miles from freedom, the Nez Perce were defeated at Snake Creek on the northern edge of the Bear Paw Mountains.

Importance

Joseph was given credit for being a great war leader and following the "white man's code of war". . . not killing or mutilating women and children. Actually Joseph was not a war chief. He took charge of the old men, women, and children. Joseph and his band held off 2,000 regulars and volunteers in a 1,700-mile retreat involving four battles and many small fights, in a campaign that lasted 120 days, from June until October. With the surrender of Joseph's Nez Perce tribe in 1877 the military conquest of the Native Americans was complete.

Focus on the Story

1. Understand the Story

Find out. Read the question. Find the answer in the story. Write it on the line.

1. Who was Joseph? _____

_____

2. What started the fight between the Nez Perce and the soldiers? _____

_____

*T*ell General Howard I know his heart. What he told me before I have in my heart. I am tired of fighting. Our chiefs are killed. Looking Glass is dead. Toohoolhoolzote is dead. The old men are all dead. It is the young men who say yes or no. He who led the young men is dead. It is cold and we have no blankets. The little children are freezing to death. My people, some of them, have run away to the hills, and have no blankets, no food; no one knows where they are—perhaps freezing to death. I want to have time to look for my children and see how many I can find. Maybe I shall find them among the dead. Hear me, my chiefs, I am tired; my heart is sick and sad. From where the sun now stands, I will fight no more forever."

— *Chief Joseph*

3. Why did the Nez Perce run away from the soldiers? _____

_____

4. Why were the Nez Perce so successful in escaping from the soldiers? _____

_____

5. Where were they going, hoping to find safety from the army? _____

_____

6. What happened in the end? _____

_____

2. Practice Vocabulary

Choose the word or definition that is closest in meaning to the word or phrases in **boldface.**

block	scouts	hostile	wilderness
slipped away	mourning	equipment	be ashamed

1. General Howard had a lot of **heavy things** to fight with.
2. The soldiers at Fort Fizzle put up a fence to **stop** the Nez Perce.
3. The Nez Perce **left quietly** without being noticed.
4. In wartime, it is necessary to have **people who look for the enemy.**
5. Chief Joseph said he would **not be proud** if he attacked sleeping people.
6. The places that were most difficult were **areas with no roads.**
7. Most settlers thought that all Indians were **unfriendly.**
8. After the battle the people were **crying for** all their dead.

3. Talk About It

Discuss these questions with a partner or in a small group:
1. Was the U.S. government right in taking the land away? Explain.
2. How are the tribal ways with nature different from the white man's?
3. Talk about the movies you have seen that show Native Americans. How are the people presented?
4. What if the Nez Perce had escaped to Canada? What would have happened to them?
5. Which side was more noble? The Nez Perce or the U.S. Army? Why?

4. Write What You Think

1. You are a newspaper reporter. Write about part of the flight of this tribe. What **bias** will you have? (Ask your teacher to explain **bias**.)
2. You are a Nez Perce survivor. Write about your feelings during the surrender.
3. You are one of the soldiers chasing the Nez Perce. Choose a day during the chase and write about it in your journal.
4. Write a new ending to this story. You could use the discussion from Section 3, number 4 on page 72.

5. Play the Part

Choose a situation below. Plan a dialogue between the characters and act it out.
1. **Joseph, Alokut.** Joseph wants to make peace. Alokut says they must fight or run.
2. **Joseph, his wife.** She wants to go on the reservation. He says they must stay with the tribe.
3. **Sarah, Morning Song.** The daughter wants to stay with the mother. The mother says she should go back and live on the reservation.
4. **Joseph, Looking Glass.** Joseph wants to keep going. Looking Glass says they will rest for a few days.
5. **Joseph, Alokut, Looking Glass.** They have different ideas about how to fight or run.
6. **Joseph, Colonel Miles, General Howard.** They discuss the terms of surrender.

6. Geography Focus

Use the map below to answer the questions.

1. Trace the trail of the Nez Perce from the Wallowa Valley to the Bear Paw battleground.

2. Which state are the Bear Paw Mountains in? _____

3. Which state is the Wallowa Valley in? _____

4. Did the Nez Perce go north, south, east, or west? _____

5. How many miles did they travel between stops? _____
   Create a scale to show the distances.

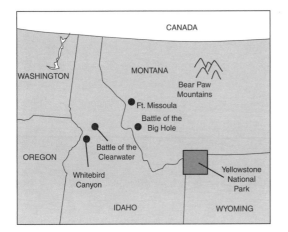

The San Francisco Earthquake of 1906

BEFORE YOU READ

Answer the following questions.

1. Have you ever been in a natural disaster? a flood? an **earthquake?** a **hurricane?** a fire?

2. What would you do if you were in an **earthquake?** Are there any safety rules?

Words to Understand

Read the sentences. Discuss what the words in **boldface** mean.

Words about Earthquakes and Other Natural Disasters

1. An **earthquake** is short, rapid vibrations of the surface of the earth.
2. The **Richter scale** is used to measure how big an **earthquake** is. A measure of 8 is very dangerous.
3. Each **tremor** or shock of the **earthquake** lasted 30 seconds, and the **earthquake** caused a sound like a **rumble** and a **roar.**
4. Many countries sent **relief** to the **earthquake refugees,** and the Army came in to **keep order,** to make the city safe.
5. **Hurricanes** are big storms that start on the sea but sometimes come onto land.

Words About People

1. He called all his **relatives:** sisters, brothers, cousins.
2. He didn't want to go, but she **talked** him **into** going to the park.
3. The men in San Francisco went to the **saloons** to drink and play cards; not many of them were **religious** or went to church or temple.
4. After something sad happens, people need to be **cheered up.**

Active Vocabulary Learning Activity

Work in pairs on a word or phrase your teacher gives you. Try to show or illustrate it. For example, if your phrase is "shoot arrows," you can say the phrase and at the same time make the physical motion of "shooting an arrow." If you wish, you can also make some gesture or facial expression related to the vocabulary.

Finally, repeat the word or the phrase and action with the class. Here are the words to use in this story:

> rumble, roar, keep order, talked into, religious, cheer up, twisting.

*T*he earth has weak points where **earthquakes** are most likely to happen. San Francisco was built on one of these weak points, the San Andreas fault. This fault runs almost the length of California's coastal mountains. This story is told by a young Hispanic girl named Alma who lived in San Francisco at that time.

The San Francisco Earthquake of 1906

The Big Shake

The horses next door made noise. What was the **rumble** I felt? The bed was moving. I jumped up and ran to the hall. Everything was shaking. Boom! The great mirror in the hall crashed to the floor. I heard a **rumble** and a **roar.** It sounded like a train coming at full speed or like wagons crossing a bridge.
5   It was still dark, and I was afraid.

"Alma, where are you?" my mother called. I couldn't find her. Then a second shock hit. The room was **twisting,** back and forth. Everything came crashing down, and I went crashing down with the house.

"Alma, Alma," my father called. I woke up. It was light. Was it a bad dream?
10   "Daddy, the walls are gone. The roof too." I went to the window, but I was at the **attic** window, and the attic window was now right above the street.

"Here, Alma," said my father as he lifted me through the window to the sidewalk, right from the attic. "The house has fallen down."

My grandmother hugged me. "Alma, it was an **earthquake,**" she said. That
15   day, April 18, 1906, became famous for us in San Francisco. The first **tremor** lasted 30 seconds; the second one lasted 25 seconds. Years later, this **earthquake** was guessed to measure 8 on the **Richter scale.**

I ran to kiss my sister, Baby Carmen. "We're all safe." said my mother.

We sat in the street, the safest place to be. Strange people walked by. "Papa,
20   look at that man. He's wearing a tuxedo jacket and pajamas and three hats, one on top of the other."

Strange Things Everywhere

My sister laughed, "Look, the bird." It was true. A woman in a nightgown was carrying a birdcage. Everyone looked **confused.**

My mother said, "Let's find some shoes. There is broken glass everywhere."

20   Suddenly I thought of our dog. "Where's Chico?"

"Chico! Chico! Chico!" Mother and I went to the back, but no Chico.

"I'm sorry, Alma," said my mother.

"The quake's over," said my father. "But look at the smoke." The city was on fire. Electric lines caused fires. Gas from the broken pipes caused fires.

25 Overturned lamps caused fires. In a half hour, 52 fires were reported.

Flames were everywhere. A fireman was across the street. "Sorry. There's no water in the pipes. All the pipes that bring water into the city are broken. You must go toward the sea." What a bad surprise! The city would burn.

"The safest place will be Golden Gate Park," my grandmother said. We

35 went in and out of our broken house, putting things into our wagon. We found mattresses, blankets, pillows, clothes, pots, pans, and unbroken dishes. Mother loaded all the food supplies: flour, sugar, beans, rice, bacon, potatoes, carrots. I brought books and my diary. I'm a writer.

We brought family pictures and Grandma Ada's portrait. Grandmother

40 **talked** Papa **into** putting her piano on the back of the wagon. "We'll need **cheering up.**" Soon, our horse was pulling the wagon to the park.

To the Park

We joined the line of homeless people heading west toward the ocean. The fire was behind us. I looked for Chico down every street. "Chico, where are you? Here, Chico." I called and called, but no luck. I feared he was dead.

45 "But what if he's hurt and looking for us? I must find him," I said to mother.

SOURCE: Culver Pictures

Earthquake refugees recover in Golden Gate Park.

The park was filled with people, many looked lost.

"Alma, help me put up our tent," said Papa. It was the same tent he used for fishing trips.

A tall sailor came to help us. "The mayor's closed the **saloons** in town, one thousand of them," he told my father.

After that I went looking for Chico again. "Chico. Chico."

"Who's Chico?" asked a tall boy.

"He's my dog," I said.

This boy was Felipe Lopez. He told me, "General Funston brought the soldiers to **keep order.** He wired Washington, D.C., to send tents and food for 20,000 people. That's how many people are homeless." Felipe was a **'know-it-all,'** but kind of nice.

Camping in the Park

Felipe and I looked for Chico. We climbed Strawberry Hill, the highest point in the park. "Look at that. The city looks like a sea of liquid fire," I said.

"Look at those giant clouds of smoke," said Felipe. The smoke clouds hung above the city for hours, and then started moving over us toward the ocean. That fire lasted three days.

Back at the park entrance, I found my family by following the music. A young man was playing **religious** songs on our piano.

"Alma, go get some soup. You haven't eaten all day." said my grandmother.

"You're right. I am hungry." The ladies had made big pots of soup. It smelled good. I stood in line for soup. In another line people signed in so that lost **relatives** could find them. I sat down with a hot bowl of vegetable and bean soup.

The soup smelled so good. Then I heard a "yip, yip" behind me. I couldn't believe it! It was Chico running toward me and the smell of food. His tail was waving. He had found us.

That was all months ago. Some people say 500 died in that quake; others say 2,000. **Relief** food and money arrived from everywhere, by ship and train. Of foreign nations, Japan sent the most.

For weeks we stood in line for food, rich and poor. Things have settled down now. I go to school in a tent in the park. We're living in a little cottage— a **refugee** shack they call it. My father is rebuilding our house. He says more than 20,000 new buildings will go up to replace those shaken and burned down. He says, "You can't hold San Francisco down."

Importance

A wild city since the Gold Rush of 1849, San Francisco became a little more conservative after 1906. The city has a Victorian look because so many buildings were built all at the same time right after the quake. The 1906 **earthquake** damaged houses along the coast from 100 miles north of San Francisco to Monterey, 100 miles south, in a path 20 to 40 miles wide.

Focus on the Story

I. Understand the Story

With a partner, scan the story for answers to these questions. (Scanning means to look over something for particular answers.)

1. What time of the day or night did the earthquake start?
2. How many shocks were there?
3. What was the date of this earthquake?
4. Where was the safest place right after the earthquake?
5. What was the new danger after the quake was over?
6. What did Alma realize was lost?
7. What was the safe place the family headed for?
8. What was the strangest thing the family took with them?
9. What did the mayor of the city close down?
10. Why were the soldiers called in?
11. What did Alma and Felipe look at when they climbed Strawberry Hill?
12. What was Alma doing when she saw Chico?
13. How many people died in the quake?
14. How did Alma describe Felipe?

Enrico Caruso, the famous opera singer, performed in San Francisco the night before the quake. When it hit, he grabbed his autographed picture of President Theodore Roosevelt and ran to the door. When he saw the orchestra director of the opera company, he threw his arms around the man and said, "I've lost my voice." The director told him to sing an aria; he did. Then he said, "I want nothing more to do with this place." He packed up, wrapped a towel around his throat, and went down to the hotel lobby and across the bay in a boat to catch a train. He never returned to San Francisco.

2. Practice Vocabulary

Choose the word or definition that is closest in meaning to the word(s) in **boldface.**

cheering up	rumble and roar	twisted	hurricane
refugees	keeping order	confused	relatives

1. Her **family** wanted to care for the old grandmother.
2. The San Francisco people needed **to be made happier.**
3. After the hurricane, people near the water were **people without homes.**
4. Alma heard a deep **noise.**
5. Young teachers sometimes have a hard time **making people behave** in the classroom.
6. A quake is as damaging as a **big storm.**
7. During the earthquake, the house **turned around,** like a big rope.
8. After the earthquake many people were **uneasy.**

3. Finish the Sentences

Draw a line between the two parts to make a correct sentence.

1. The quake was guessed to measure
2. Alma looked for
3. The fire destroyed
4. The piano
5. The earthquake covered
6. The homeless people

a. stayed in the park.
b. 200 miles of the California coast.
c. cheered them up.
d. 8 on the Richter Scale.
e. her dog Chico.
f. most of San Francisco.

4. Talk About It

Discuss these questions with a partner or in a small group:

1. Would you prefer living in 1900 or in 2000? Why?
2. What was happening in other countries in the years between 1900 and 1910?
3. What other cities have had major **earthquakes** in the 20th century?
4. How old do you think Alma (the narrator) is?

5. Write What You Think

1. Write a newspaper article for an eastern city or for an article in a foreign newspaper.
2. Write a story about the **earthquake** from Felipe's viewpoint.
3. Write a letter from Enrico Caruso to a friend, telling about his stay in San Francisco.
4. Write a summary of the story. Include all the main points.

6. Play the Part

Choose a situation below. Plan a dialogue between the characters and act it out.

1. **Alma, her mother.** Alma wants to go back into the burning city to look for Chico.
2. **Alma's grandmother, her father.** She wants to bring the piano, he says no.
3. **General Funston, the mayor.** The mayor wants to be boss; General Funston says that he is the boss.
4. **Alma, her father.** She wants to move to the top of Strawberry Hill; he says she has to stay with the family.
5. **Felipe, Alma.** He wants to quit school; Alma says he needs to stay in school.
6. **Grandmother, Alma.** They talk about **earthquake** problems and fears.

7. Story Theater

1. Work with a group of students.
2. Choose a section of the story with the class.
3. Read the section with your group. With your group decide which role you will play. If possible, change everything to conversation. Feel free to change the description to conversation. Choose any props you wish.
4. Practice your section for 15–20 minutes with your group.
5. Perform your story for the class. Try to make the story theater flow from one part to the next.

Chapter 11

Roosevelts

BEFORE YOU READ

Answer the following questions.

1. Have you had a limitation, a **handicap,** in your life? Is anyone in your family handicapped?

2. What do you know about Franklin Delano Roosevelt (FDR) and his wife Eleanor?

Words to Understand

Read the sentences. Discuss what the words in **boldface** mean.

Words About Illness

1. FDR got sick with **polio,** a disease, and it **paralyzed** his legs.
2. FDR was **handicapped**; he couldn't walk without **crutches** or a **cane.**
3. To overcome this handicap, he tried many **therapies** but found no **remedy** for his problem.
4. His mother said he should retire, not work, and be an **invalid.**

Words About Families

1. Oftentimes, an **adolescent** has unexpected emotional **outbursts.**
2. Eleanor Roosevelt had been a **traditional** wife, willing to give in to her **domineering** mother-in-law, Sara Roosevelt.
3. The Roosevelt family was wealthy and had a large **estate** near New York City.

Words About Emotional Difficulty

1. Eleanor **fell apart** and could not stop **sobbing.**
2. After her outburst she wanted to **pull herself together.**
3. Her **going to pieces** was probably caused by the **stress** of her husband's sickness.
4. It was difficult for Eleanor to **control her temper** and **stand up to** Sara when they disagreed.
5. Eleanor's **break down** helped her daughter Anna to go to her with her problems.
6. Eleanor **recovered** quickly from all the arguments.

Active Vocabulary Learning Activity

Work in pairs on a word or phrase your teacher gives you. Try to show or illustrate it. For example, if your phrase is "shoot arrows," you can say the phrase and at the same time make the physical motion of "shooting an arrow." If you wish, you can also make some gesture or facial expression related to the vocabulary.

Finally, repeat the word or the phrase and action with the class. Here are the words to use in this story:

break down, fell apart, recover, control her temper, sobbing, domineering, paralyzed, stand up to, struggle, crutches, stress.

*F*ranklin Delano Roosevelt (1882–1945) was the only American president elected four times. When he was 38, in 1920, he ran for vice president, but in 1921 it looked like he would never be a leader again. He got **polio,** and his legs were **paralyzed.** Until that time his wife, Eleanor Roosevelt, niece of another American president, Teddy Roosevelt, had been content to be a **traditional** wife, raising her six children, staying in the background, and avoiding publicity. Franklin's mother, Sara, was a strong-willed woman, and Eleanor had always done what the older woman wanted. Louis Howe, FDR's assistant, was also important to FDR's recovery. This story is told by Eleanor.

The Roosevelts

He Will Not Walk Again

A few months after my husband, Franklin Roosevelt, got sick with polio, we moved him into our house in New York City. My mother-in-law, Sara, lived next door. She and I had daily arguments about what was best for Franklin.

"Franklin will never walk again. We must move him back to our **estate** in
5 the country," said Sara.

"But, mother Sara, that is wrong. He wants to continue his political career," I said.

"He can't. That is ridiculous. He is **paralyzed.** He will never walk, no matter how hard he tries," said Sara.

10 "We don't know that yet," I said. "He wants to try all the new **therapies.**"

SOURCE: Corbis-Bettmann

Isolating polio victims helped keep the disease from spreading.

"I can't allow it. He is too weak and it is too dangerous. I worry that he might get sick again. He must accept that he is an **invalid,**" said Sara. "He must **retire** and enjoy the life of a country gentleman. Even if he is **paralyzed,** he can be comfortable and protected, much like his own father was. I have made up my mind."

"But mother Sara, it is important to do what Franklin wants." I had to **control my temper** and not fight with Franklin's willful mother, who was used to getting everything she wanted. "His doctor wants him to be active; we must try to do what the doctor says."

"Eleanor, he's my son. I know what is best for him," said Sara.

I left the room in tears.

In the hall my daughter Anna stopped me. She was angry too. "Mother, why should I have the small room? You gave a much nicer room to Mr. Howe. Why do you treat him better than you treat me?"

"Oh, Anna, Mr. Howe needs that large room to help your father with his work. You're still a child, and at least you have a room of your own," I said.

"Oh, mother, I'm 15 years old, and I think I should be treated better. My friends say I should have the better room. You don't consider me. I don't think you care about me."

Everyone in Tears

With that, Anna ran in tears to her small room at the back of the house. I didn't tell her that I didn't have a room at all; I was sleeping on a bed in her baby brother's room.

Later I realized that as an **adolescent** girl, she needed more consideration. I still thought of her as a child and was treating her like a child. She needed to be taken into my confidence, for me to talk with her about our difficulties, not just make rules for her to obey. She needed to understand her father and all he was fighting against.

When I had **recovered** from these arguments with my mother-in-law and my daughter, I went to Franklin's room.

"Your mother wants you to retire to the country," I said.

"Never. I will walk again, and I will go back to work. You will see, dear. I am getting stronger every day," said Franklin.

"I don't know what to do. Your mother disagrees with you, with me, with Dr. Draper. He says it is better for you to take an active part in life again and lead, as far as possible, a normal life," I said.

"My mother is wrong this time. I will get better, and I will go back into politics," said Franklin.

Louis Howe knocked on the door and entered. He had been Franklin's assistant for years. His presence in the house helped me to **stand up to** Franklin's mother. This was the first time in my 20 years of married life that I was able to disagree successfully with her. She was a very **domineering** woman. Mr. Howe helped Franklin and me to direct our lives during the years following the polio attack.

I Will Walk Again

"Louis, I am certain I will walk again," said Franklin. "I am determined to seek
55 any **remedy** and follow any plan of action that offers hope."

"Good! I know you can do it. You're stretching your leg muscles now. The
doctor says it could bring life back into them," said Louis.

These exercises were very painful to Franklin, but he never complained or
seemed discouraged. He didn't want to be a helpless individual. Slowly, the use
60 of his hands and arms came back completely, and he developed broad shoulders
and strong arms, but his legs remained useless.

This was the most difficult winter of my life. My mother-in-law thought
we were tiring my husband and that he should be completely quiet. Our
discussions about his care became daily arguments.

65 Finally, I **broke down.** One day I was reading a story to the youngest
boys, and I found myself **sobbing** as I read. I could not stop. Other people
came in the room and tried to stop me, but nothing worked. I cried for hours.
Eventually I left the room and found an empty room to **pull myself together.**
This sort of emotional **outburst** requires an audience, as a rule, to keep it up,
70 so I was able to stop when I was alone. This is the only time I remember in
my whole life that I **fell apart** and **went to pieces** in this way.

The outburst did have a good effect on Anna, however, because she came
to me later and talked about her problems, and we were able to become
close again.

75 That same week I met with Louis Howe. "Mrs. Roosevelt, to keep your
husband's interest alive, we must keep him in contact with politics," he said.

"This seems like an impossible task. He is so weak right now," I said.

Until 1945 Eleanor Roosevelt was known for being the wife of FDR, but she became famous in her own right after his death. The next president asked her to represent her country as a delegate to the United Nations. There she was a force in creating the Universal Declaration of Human Rights. She was the humanitarian spirit at its best and was called "the First Lady of the World," a person who walked with kings but also had the common touch.

Keep the Roosevelt Name in the Public Eye

"Also, we must keep the Roosevelt name in the public eye,"
he said.

80 "Louis, how can we do that? Franklin is still recovering,
and he can't be seen in this helpless condition. People don't
forget and would never vote for him again," I said.

"Eleanor, your name is Roosevelt too. You can be a
stand-in to maintain the **visibility** of the Roosevelt name,"
85 said Louis.

"But I'm no politician. What can I do?" I asked.

"You must do some political work again, perhaps with the
New York State Democratic party," said Louis.

Right then I could think of nothing to do, but later that
90 year a friend invited me to help raise funds for the
Democratic Party. After doing this, I went to work with the
Democratic Women of New York State. I was seen
and heard, and the Roosevelt name was not forgotten.

"Life has got to be lived—that's all there is to it."
QUOTATION BY ELEANOR ROOSEVELT

All that year, my husband **struggled** to do many things that would help
95 him to be more active, like using crutches to walk every day to gain confidence.
Each new thing took determination and great physical effort. Little by little,
he learned to walk, first with **crutches** and then with a **cane,** leaning on
someone's arm. But for the rest of his life, he could not walk alone.

The difficult part about his not being able to walk was that it had to be
100 hidden in public. We didn't think the people wanted to be led by a man
who could not walk.

Franklin learned to live a normal life. On the whole, his general physical
condition improved year by year, until he was stronger in some ways than
before his illness. He became an **inspiration** to all people who must overcome
105 a life-changing challenge.

Importance

Three years after his polio attack, FDR was able to give a nominating speech
at the Democratic Convention in 1924. FDR is usually remembered for three
things: for actively working to get the country out of the Great Depression in
the 1930s through work projects, for leading the United States during World
War II, and for being elected four times. But for some people, he is most important as an **inspiration.** He had the courage and persistence to recover
from his sickness and rise to great national office and achievement.

Focus on the Story

I. Understand the Story

Making your own questions. Go through the story, section by section, and
make 10–15 questions about the important ideas in this story. Do this alone,
in a pair, or in a group of three. Afterwards, you could pass them to another
person or group and see if they can answer them.

Example: How was FDR paralyzed?

2. Practice Vocabulary

Use these words to complete the sentences:

inspiration   struggled   stand in   visible
fell apart   lose her temper   stand up to   retire

1. Louis Howe told Eleanor, "You can _____ for your husband."

2. FDR is an _____ for many people who have a handicap.

3. He _____ to learn to walk with the help of crutches or a cane.

4. Sara wanted him to _____ to live on their estate in the country.

5. Eleanor _____ under the difficulties of the family problems.

6. She didn't want to _____ when she argued with her mother-in-law.

7. She learned to _____ Sara about Franklin's care.

8. Eleanor worked to keep the Roosevelt name _____ to the public.

3. Make Inferences

To make an inference, we combine what we see and hear with what we already know (background knowledge) to make conclusions (inferences) about a character or situation in stories. In this exercise many answers may be right.

> **Example:** Make an inference about how a traditional wife like
> Eleanor Roosevelt acts.
> She is primarily a homemaker and doesn't express opinions.

1. **He Will Not Walk Again:** Make an inference about why mother Sara wants to limit Franklin's efforts.
2. **Everyone in Tears:** Make an inference about why Louis Howe's presence in the house helped Eleanor.
3. **I Will Walk Again:** Make an inference about Franklin's personality or character.
4. **Keep the Roosevelt Name in the Public Eye:** Make an inference about why Eleanor thought people wouldn't want to be led by a man in a wheelchair.

4. Talk About It

Discuss these questions with a partner or in a small group:
1. Does a physical handicap make it difficult to be elected? Why? Why not?
2. Explain all the challenges someone with paralyzed legs must overcome.
3. Why did Eleanor have problems getting along with Sara Roosevelt?
4. What were Eleanor's difficulties with her daughter Anna?
5. How did Eleanor help her husband's future?

5. Write What You Think

1. Write a summary of the story.
2. Write a diary entry by any of the people in the Roosevelt home.
3. Write a newspaper story about FDR's comeback to politics in 1924.
4. Write a letter from Franklin to his best friend at this time of his life.

6. Play the Part

Choose a situation below. Plan a dialogue between the characters and act it out.
1. **Eleanor, Sara.** They argue about Franklin's care.
2. **Eleanor, Sara.** They argue about Franklin's future.
3. **Eleanor, Anna.** Eleanor wants Anna to practice piano. Anna says no.
4. **FDR, Louis Howe.** FDR wants to go to his office. Louis says it's too soon.
5. **Anna, her brother/s.** She tells them to behave. They ask about what's wrong in the house.
6. **Sara, FDR.** She wants him to retire. He tells her no.

7. Story Theater

1. Work with a group of students.
2. Choose a section of the story with the class.
3. Read the section with your group. With your group decide which role you will play. If possible, change everything to conversation. Feel free to change the description to conversation. Choose any props you wish.
4. Practice your section for 15–20 minutes with your group.
5. Perform your story for the class. Try to make the story theater flow from one part to the next.

Chapter 12

The
Magic of Disney

BEFORE YOU READ

Answer the following questions.

1. **What does Disney mean to you? Do you know what Walt Disney did?**

2. **What do you know about making films? making cartoons?**

Words to Understand

Read the sentences. Discuss what the words in **boldface** mean.

Words About Film

1. Walt liked to **doodle,** usually drawing humorous **cartoons.**
2. He worked as an artist in a **commercial art studio.**
3. Part of learning **animation** was learning how to **operate a camera.**
4. Walt drew his cartoons on paper, then traced them onto **celluloid,** a new type of plastic.
5. Cartoons were shorter than **feature films.**
6. Walt had a difficult time collecting money from the **distribution companies** that placed his cartoons in theaters.

Qualities or Traits in People

1. Walt had a **favorite** pig.
2. Walt's teachers said he didn't **pay attention** in school.
3. Mickey Mouse was **gallant** (brave and courageous).
4. Like Walt, Mickey was also **resourceful,** full of ideas.
5. Walt felt **betrayed** by his artists leaving him to work for the distribution company.

Words About Money

1. Disney **earned,** or made, money by selling his drawings.
2. Disney was willing to **risk** all his money on the new cartoons.
3. When he ran out of money, he **declared bankruptcy.**
4. Disney **hired** 300 artists to work on his first cartoon feature film, *Snow White and the Seven Dwarfs.*

Active Vocabulary Learning Activity

Work in pairs on a word or phrase your teacher gives you. Try to show or illustrate it. For example, if your phrase is "shoot arrows," you can say the phrase and at the same time make the physical motion of "shooting an arrow." If you wish, you can also make some gesture or facial expression related to the vocabulary.

Finally, repeat the word or the phrase and action with the class. Here are the words to use in this story:

resourceful, doodle, operate a camera, pay attention, favorite, gallant, earned.

This story is told by Walt Disney, who was born in 1901. The Disney name is known around the world, and represents magic and fantasy to most. Walt first became famous as a cartoonist and later influenced film in many ways. Now he is especially known as the creator of theme park entertainment. His story shows how some people react to hard times: a father's failures, early bankruptcy, trouble with business partners.

The Magic of Disney

Living on a Farm

I always loved animals. I was happiest when we moved to a farm in Missouri when I was five. My mother said, "Walt, you can take care of the chickens and pigs."

"Look, Mom, my chicken just laid an egg on my hand."

5 "Walt, get off that pig's back. I don't think Porker likes to carry you around," said my mother. I liked ducks, horses, goats, cats, and mice too.

Then one day, my brother Roy said, "Walt, let's go hunting." He shot a rabbit, and I was scared by the gunshot. Later that day, Mom cooked a rabbit **stew,** but I couldn't eat it.

10 "I don't want to hunt or kill animals," I told Roy the next time he asked me to go.

My uncle helped me find little mice. He showed me how to make them stay in my pockets and get wild birds to sit on my shoulder. In school I drew all our farm animals. I showed my best pictures to our doctor.

15 The doctor said, "Walt, I like your pictures. Would you draw a picture of Rupert, my horse?" I did, and Doc Sherwood gave me a half-dollar for the picture! That was the first time I **earned** money for my drawing.

That same year, 1910, when I was eight, all our pigs got sick, and we had to kill them, even Porker. My Dad got sick too—but, of course, we didn't kill him.
20 Roy was only 16 and couldn't do all the work, so we had to sell the farm and move to Kansas City.

School was OK, but my teachers said I didn't **pay attention.** I liked drawing, but even there I had a little trouble. "Walt," said my teacher, "I told you to draw a bowl of flowers. Why did you give each flower a face and arms?"
25 I guess I saw things differently.

I made money delivering newspapers so that I could go to movies. *Snow White* was my **favorite** film, and Charlie Chaplin was my favorite actor.

But drawing was always my favorite thing to do. I got free hair cuts by doing **cartoons** at the barber shop. When I was 14, I took art lessons at the
30 Kansas City Art Institute. I already knew I wanted to be a cartoonist, but my father said, "You'll never make a living by drawing."

We Move Again

Dad didn't do well, and we moved again, this time to Chicago. I drew cartoons for my high school newspaper, and went to the Chicago Academy of Fine Arts after school. In 1918, during World War I, I was only 16, but I
35 lied about my age and joined the service. I had spent one year in high school, and I never returned. When the war ended, I said, "I want to be an artist."

"An artist can't make any money," my father said again.

I joined my brother Roy in Kansas City and worked in a small **commercial art studio** at 18. I made a new friend, Ubbe Iwerks. When that job ended, we
40 formed our own art studio. We both loved cartoons.

"Roy," I said to my brother, "I want to learn the film-cartoon business."

"Get a job at a film advertising company," Roy suggested. I did and I learned the basics of **animation.** These ads were short cartoons for businesses that paid movie theaters to show them between **feature films.**

45 In New York City, animators were having their drawings traced on plastic material called **celluloid.** I started doing that. I drew rough pictures for a cartoon idea, and Ubbe would turn out a pile of excellent drawings in a short time.

"Ubbe, why don't we film our own cartoons?"

"Can you learn to **operate a camera?**" asked Ubbe.

50 "Yes, and we can work all day at the ad company and work at night on our own cartoons," I said.

"Let's call our company Laugh-O-gram Films," he said.

Our first cartoon was "Little Red Riding Hood." It was so good, I quit the job at the ad company and raised $15,000 to buy cameras, projectors, film, all
55 the equipment needed to produce filmed cartoons. We hired more workers and turned out seven cartoons. The films did well, but something was wrong.

What's Wrong?

"Walt, why don't we have any money?" asked Ubbe.

"Our New York **distribution company** didn't pay us. We're almost broke."

I had to move out of my apartment and into my office, where the rent had
60 been paid in advance. Roy had moved out west for his health. He gave me some money, but I missed him. I found a new friend in my time of need. A mouse appeared on my desk, and I started feeding him. This was a low point for me, but the mouse kept me company.

Then the phone rang, "Walt Disney? I'm a dentist, and I'll give you $500
65 to make a cartoon about dental health." I **risked** that $500 on another cartoon, this one with a live child and a number of cartoon animals. This was new, to make a cartoon background for a live actress. I called it "Alice."

But bad luck caught up with me. I ran out of money and **declared bankruptcy** in 1923. "Walt, you can keep the footage of the Alice film and
70 your camera," said the bank manager.

I decided to move to the West Coast, to Roy and Hollywood. But first I took the mouse to the country and let him go.

In Hollywood I started to make Alice cartoons. Roy helped, and Ubbe joined the staff. The films got good reviews, but again the distributor paid
75 slowly.

To produce early cartoons, the artists drew figures and operators then cut them out and attached them to a drawing board. The arms and legs of the figures were joined and could be placed in different positions. Cameramen moved the figures' limbs into a position, photographed the figures, then moved the limbs to a slightly different position, and photographed the figures again. The process was repeated over and over with hundreds of photos, each showing a small change of position. When the photographs were combined on a strip of film and viewed at a higher speed, the figure looked as if it were moving.

Love came next. A young woman named Lillian Bounds worked for us. In 1925 Lilly and I got married.

We started making cartoons about a rabbit named Oswald. Ubbe gave him a personality, and I sold a **series** to Universal Pictures. It did really well. Lilly
80 and I went by train to New York to sign a new Oswald contract. "I'll ask for more money," I said.

"You'll get less money," said the distributor, Charles Mintz. "And if you don't sign, we will take your artists. Your artists have already signed contracts with me."

85 "Our company owns Oswald," I said.

A Star is Born

"No, it doesn't. Universal owns Oswald," said Mintz, "and they're ready to produce the cartoon, with or without you."

I called Roy to ask if all this was true. Roy called back. "It's true. Ubbe didn't sign, but 11 of our 14 artists signed contracts with Mintz. And yes, it's
90 true. Universal does own the rights to Oswald."

I felt **betrayed.** I walked the streets of New York for hours and then returned to Mintz's office. I threw down a picture of Oswald and said, "He's all yours."

"How are you going to make money without Oswald?" Mintz asked.
95 "Don't worry," I said and pointed to my head, "There are many more characters where he came from."

On the three-day train trip going back west, I drew and **doodled.** I remembered the mouse in my office back in those lonely days. I drew a mouse with big ears, a pointed nose, and button eyes. Lilly looked at the picture and
100 smiled.

I said, "Mortimer the Mouse is his name. He will be **gallant, resourceful, mischievous.**"

"Mortimer? Umm, I don't like that name for a mouse. I think his name is Mickey. Mickey Mouse," said Lilly.
105 There on that train ride from New York, was the birth of our famous cartoon character.

Years later, after Mickey Mouse cartoons made the Disney name famous, I kept putting our company in debt with new ideas like sound, Technicolor, and feature-length cartoons. One day, Roy said, "Walt, we're in trouble.
110 We're in debt $5 million."

I started laughing. "That's really funny, Roy. We must be doing something right."

"How can you say that? I'm worried," said Roy.

"It's funny that we're in debt $5 million. I can remember a time when no
115 one would lend us $1,000. It must mean we're successful if we can borrow $5 million."

Walt Disney's ideas were usually successful; but when he conceived the idea of Disneyland Park, no one would finance it. He couldn't find the money. So he finally thought up the idea of putting his films on television and offered a new television company, ABC, the "Disneyland" show. ABC agreed, and this money financed Disneyland Park. Walt said he liked the park because it was a living thing and he could keep changing it, unlike a film that was over once it was completed.

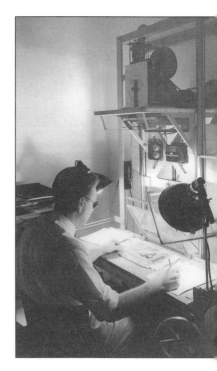

Importance

From that experience of losing Oswald, Walt was careful not to give control of his creations to any other company. In 1932 Disney was the first to use Technicolor in cartoons and won an Academy Award®. His cartoons stressed character and plot. His first full-length feature cartoon story, *Snow White and the Seven Dwarfs,* completed in 1937, won the Academy Award® for the best picture. Before it came out, people were calling it "Disney's folly" because it was such a costly production.

Focus on the Story

1. Understand the Story

With a partner, scan the story for answers to these questions. (Scanning means to look over something for particular answers.)

1. What part of the United States did Walt Disney come from?
2. Where did Walt get his love of animals?
3. Why didn't Walt finish high school?
4. Who was Roy?
5. What type of art was his first love in life?
6. Who was his first business partner?
7. What was the problem Walt had with his film distributors?
8. Why was Walt upset about the loss of the character Oswald?
9. Where did Walt find the idea for the mouse character?
10. Who named the mouse Mickey Mouse?
11. What qualities did Mickey and Walt both have?
12. Why did Walt laugh about debt? Why didn't he worry?
13. How did Walt finance his first Disney Theme Park?

2. Practice Vocabulary

Use these words to complete the sentences.

declaring bankruptcy   stew   animation   doodling
risks   betrayed   favorite   mischievous

1. Walt was always _____, making pictures of animals.

2. _____ is the art of making pictures look like they're moving.

3. Mickey Mouse remained Walt Disney's _____ character.

4. The mother made a _____ with the rabbit and vegetables.

5. When his animators signed with Mintz, Walt felt _____ by them.

6. Mickey Mouse, a character who got in trouble, was _____.

7. Walt Disney was willing and able to take big _____.

8. One time this resulted in his losing all his money and _____.

3. Make Questions from Answers

More than one question is possible.

> **Example:** At first, Walt wanted to name Mickey Mouse Mortimer.
> Here are some possible questions:
> What did Walt want to name his new mouse cartoon character?
> Who did Walt want to name Mortimer?
> Why didn't Walt call the mouse Mortimer?

1. Walt Disney lived on a farm when he was a boy.
2. Walt wanted Mickey to be gallant, resourceful, and mischievous.
3. Roy went to live in California.
4. He wanted to make cartoons.
5. Walt said he could create more characters to replace Oswald.
6. The distribution company didn't pay us for our cartoons.

4. Talk About It

Discuss these questions with a partner or in a small group:
1. What were the qualities Walt had that made him so successful?
2. Do you think it was a mistake for him not to finish high school?
3. Was Walt Disney more of a businessman or more of an artist?
4. Have you ever been to a Disney Theme Park? Discuss your reactions.
5. What do you think about debt? Is it a good thing to be able to borrow money?

5. Write What You Think

1. Choose a Disney character and describe him or her as fully as you can.
2. Write about business and about why some businesses succeed and others don't.
3. Write a summary of the story. Include all major points.

6. Play the Part

Choose a situation below. Plan a dialogue between the characters and act it out.
1. **Walt, his mom.** Walt wants to go to war. She doesn't want him to go.
2. **Walt, his dad.** Walt wants to be an artist. His dad disagrees.
3. **Walt, Roy.** Walt wants to spend money on Disneyland Park. Roy says it will cost too much.
4. **Walt, Mintz.** Walt wants Mintz to give him the money. Mintz says he owns Oswald.
5. **Lilly, Roy.** Lilly says Walt works too much. Roy disagrees.
6. **Walt, Ubbe.** They disagree about something about their cartoon characters.

7. Artistic Response

On a piece of paper, draw a picture, cartoons, or a mind map responding to this story. Use any kind of visual response to the story that you can imagine. Then take turns explaining your art in small groups or to the class.

Chapter 13

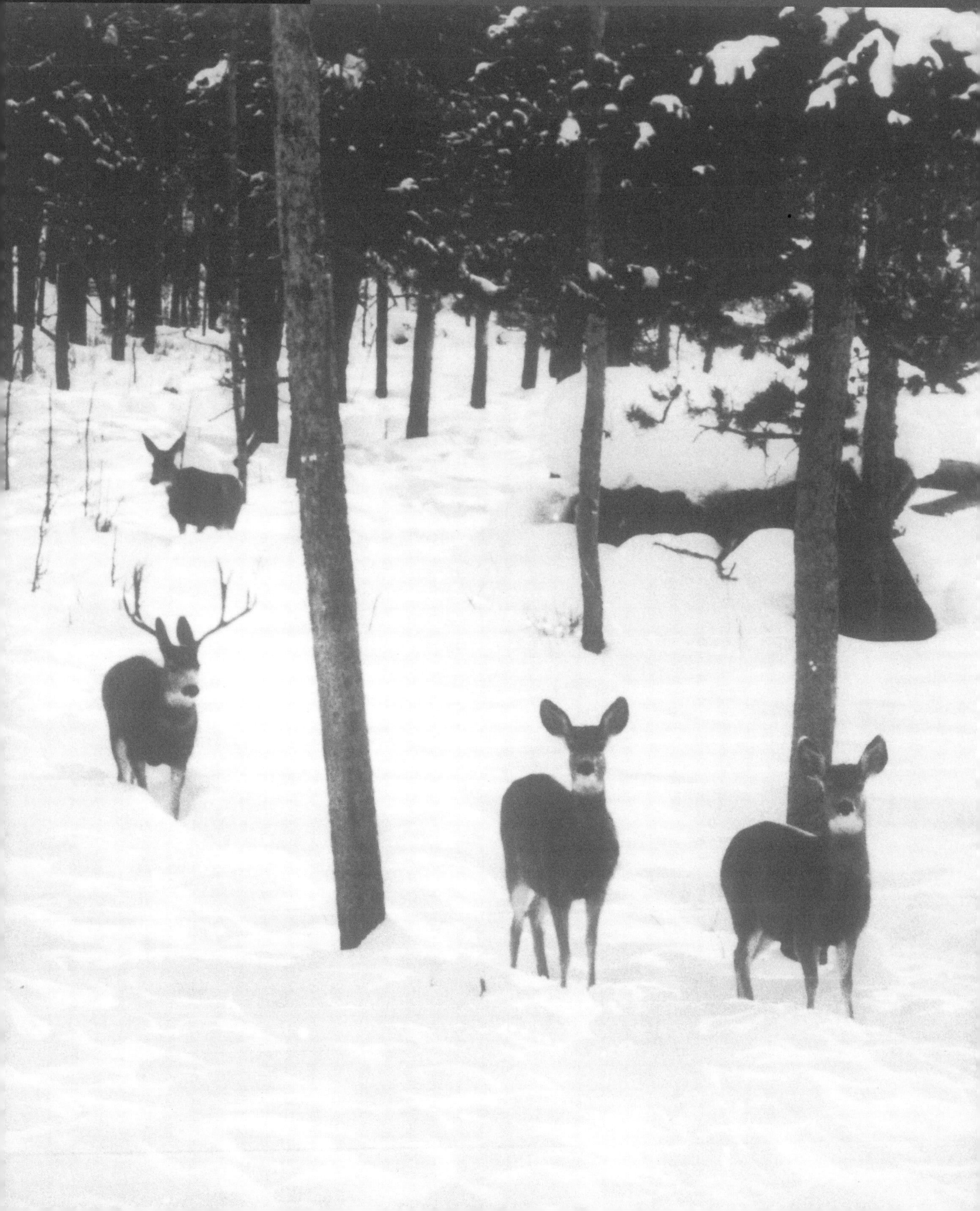

The
Web of Life

BEFORE YOU READ

Answer the following questions.

1. What is **ecology?**

2. In what ways are people harming the earth?

3. Name some **endangered** parts of life on earth.

4. What is a **web?**

Words to Understand

Read the sentences. Discuss what the words in **boldface** mean.

Words About Ecology and Preserving Nature

1. **Conservation** makes our **natural resources** last longer.
2. **Ecology** teaches that all species are **interdependent.**
3. **Ecologists** see humans as part of nature in a **web** of life.
4. When a species overpopulates, it sometimes destroys its **habitat.**
5. Many **species** of animals are **endangered,** and others are now **extinct.**

Words About Wolves and Deer

1. Wolves live in groups, called **packs.** They return to the same **dens.**
2. If there are no **predators,** like wolves, then deer can **overpopulate** to the point of unhealthy **excess.**
3. Young wolf cubs have no **caution** and don't fear the **scent,** or smell, of man.
4. A **bounty** is a reward given to a hunter for killing or catching a certain animal.

Active Vocabulary Learning Activity

Work in pairs on a word or phrase your teacher gives you. Try to show or illustrate it. For example, if your phrase is "shoot arrows," you can say the phrase and at the same time make the physical motion of "shooting an arrow." If you wish, you can also make some gesture or facial expression related to the vocabulary.

Finally, repeat the word or the phrase and action with the class. Here are the words to use in this story:

scent, conservation, binoculars, predators, interdependent, caution, extinct, excess.

*I*n 1900 some thoughtful people began to see the limits of North America's **natural resources.** Until this time, there was no limit to the destruction from unregulated hunting and fishing, logging, mining, plowing. The necessity of **conservation** became clear, but this concern over the health of the planet was new. **Ecology,** the study of how all parts of the earth affect the whole, is a word first used in the 1930s. According to the older scientific view, nature is a collection of bits of matter. The **ecological** view sees it as a **web,** and if you disturb one part, the whole is changed. This story is about one early ecologist, Aldo Leopold, who worked in the Forest Service and was a professor in forestry education. Over a long life of observation, he realized that all of nature is **interdependent.** This story shows one of his main battles, how to deal with the overpopulation of a species.

The Web of Life

The Hunter Follows the Wolf

The hunter walked slowly through the forest, listening, listening. He heard soft steps ahead. Could it be a wolf? The state pays me $100 for every wolf I kill, he thought. Maybe I can follow the wolf to his den and kill several of them. Where there's one, there will be more because wolves live in **packs,**
5 not alone. That means I'll get more money.

At the same time across this small valley stood Aldo Leopold, a **conservationist** who understood the **ecology** of the area.

Leopold looked through his **binoculars,** and he saw the hunter. He said to his assistant, "Peter, can you see the hunter on that hill? It's too early for deer
10 hunters. What do you think he's doing?"

Peter looked across the valley. "Look, Professor, ahead of him. There's a wolf pup on the trail, near that pine tree. The hunter is following the pup. I bet that man is a **bounty** hunter," said Peter.

"He probably doesn't know we removed the bounty on wolves. Hunters can't
15 kill wolves anymore. They're almost **extinct** in this area. We'd better hurry over there and tell him."

They talked as they walked. "Professor, why are all these young pine trees dying?"

The Trees Tell the Story

"These young trees have been eaten and killed by the deer. The deer are hurting
20 the forest," said Leopold.

"Why are the deer eating the trees?" asked Peter.

"They've **overpopulated** their areas, and they're destroying their **habitat.** Without **predators,** like wolves, the forces of nature aren't balanced, and the deer are too plentiful for this area."

The two men were walking through the forest, gathering information about young trees. They worked for the conservation office in Wisconsin. They reported on the condition of new tree growth.

The conservation office needed to know about the changes in the forest.

As the two men crossed the valley, Peter asked his teacher about conservation policy. "Professor, I don't understand why the state paid men to kill wolves, mountain lions, and other **predators.**"

"For a long time, conservationists thought only of increasing wildlife for hunters to kill. They didn't think about other uses for the forest. They wanted to provide deer for the hunters to kill every year. In my younger days, 30 years ago, I encouraged hunters to kill predators, but I didn't know about the possible results. I didn't realize that the deer population would grow too large if we removed the predators. I thought there would never be too many deer."

We Don't Kill Wolves Anymore

"Yes, professor, I understand. I see now what happens when there are no predators to control the deer. They overpopulate. Then they destroy their own habitat, killing many tree species. There are no little trees because the deer ate them," said Peter.

On the hill ahead the hunter slowed down when he saw the wolf pup. Oh, it's a pup, he thought. Even better. He's too young to recognize my **scent.** I can follow closely.

"He's following the pup." Leopold wanted to shout "Stop" to the man but knew his voice wouldn't be heard across the valley. "We'd better hurry over there and prevent his killing any wolves. It might be the last pack in this area. Last year I noticed a wolf **den** just over that hill." Wolves use the same dens year after year.

The hunter was only 20 feet behind the light gray pup when the pup suddenly lay down and started scratching himself. When he saw the hunter, he ran over to him, barking, thinking it was an animal to play with. Because wolf pups lead protected lives, this pup was not afraid of a man. It takes months for them to learn **caution.** This pup was lost, separated from his family.

The hunter stopped. "Should I shoot him and at least get $100?" he asked himself. He raised the rifle to his shoulder. The pup sat back on his hind legs, tilted his head and looked up at the hunter with questioning eyes.

The hunter thought, I can't shoot that small trusting animal. He looks too much like my dog, Sadie! The pup turned around and padded happily up the trail. The hunter started to follow again.

Too Many Deer

Just then Leopold and Peter caught up with the hunter. "Young man. What are you doing?" asked Leopold. The wolf pup hurried away.

"You just lost me a bounty. What's wrong with you?" yelled the hunter.

"The state conservation office no longer pays bounties to kill wolves," said Leopold.

"I don't believe you. Who are you?" said the hunter.

"Didn't you hear? We know now that the wolves save the forest. They keep the deer from overpopulating."

"That's crazy. We'll never have too many deer. It just means we can hunt
70 more," said the hunter.

"This area has too many deer now. Look at these tiny trees. The deer are eating or killing them." Leopold said. "We need the wolves because they limit the deer."

"Why can't we let the hunters kill the **excess** deer?" asked the man.

75 "It's complicated." Leopold explained the chain of animals and trees in the forest. After an hour of walking and talking, the man began to understand.

Aldo Leopold kept talking, hoping he could convince one more person to think about the big picture of nature, the **interdependence** of all living things, the **web** of life.

Importance

Aldo Leopold promoted a state of harmony between people and land. Some believe that his "harmony-with-nature" philosophy of conservation is the only 20th century North American philosophy that might work in the 21st century. He believed that ecosystem or land health is the "capacity of the land for self-renewal." He wanted to provide all the earth's species with enough living space.

Leopold spent many hours studying the forest ecosystem with his dog, Flip.

Focus on the Story

1. Understand the Story

Find out. Read the question. Find the answer in the story. Write it on the line.

Example: Why is the hunter in the forest?
He wants to kill a wolf and collect money for it.

1. Why are Aldo Leopold and Peter in the forest? _____

   _____

2. How are the deer hurting the forest? _____

   _____

3. What has caused the deer to overpopulate? _____

   _____

4. Why does Leopold say that wolves and other predators are needed in the forest? _____

   _____

5. How did giving money (bounties) to hunters hurt the forest? _____

   _____

2. Practice Vocabulary

Choose the word or definition that is closest in meaning to the word(s) in
boldface.

becoming extinct	excessive	habitat	caution
are interdependent	scent	packs	conservation

1. **Saving natural resources** was popular before the science of ecology was named.
2. Young wolf cubs are protected and have no **fear** about others.
3. Wolves live in **groups** and usually mate for life.
4. All animals have a certain **smell.**
5. Ecologists teach that all species **depend on each other.**
6. The deer were overpopulating and destroying their own **home area.**
7. These days, there are many species at risk of **disappearing forever.**
8. The deer were overpopulating and becoming **too many** for the area.

3. Cause and Effect

Complete each sentence by choosing the right cause. The first part of the sentence is the effect, the end result.

Example: The hunter was following the wolf cub because
- a. the hunter liked to walk.
- b. he loved wolves.
- (c.) he wanted to kill the wolves for money.

1. The trees were being eaten by the deer because
   - a. young trees are poisonous.
   - b. the deer had eaten all their normal food in the area.
   - c. there were too many trees.
2. A species, like deer, will overpopulate
   - a. if its natural enemy, or predator, is killed off in that area.
   - b. if there is not enough food.
   - c. if there are too many predators (such as wolves.)
3. Wolves were almost extinct in the area of the story because
   - a. wolves are not healthy animals.
   - b. the deer killed them.
   - c. there was a bounty on wolves, and hunters had killed most of them.
4. Ecology teaches that all species are important because
   - a. they are interrelated, and the biosystem depends on all types of life.
   - b. they might have a cure for cancer.
   - c. they have financial value.

4. Talk About It

Discuss these questions with a partner or in a small group.
1. Why has ecology become a popular subject?
2. Is it possible to save the earth as a pleasant healthy planet for future generations? How?
3. What can you do to help the natural world?
4. What species of animals or birds are in danger of extinction?
5. Are some countries more active than others in protecting the environment? Why?

5. Write What You Think

1. Describe other environmental concerns besides the extinction of species.
2. Write a letter to an editor, calling for action about an environmental problem in your area.
3. Imagine you are a newspaper reporter and interview Aldo Leopold, discussing environmental problems.

6. Play the Part

Choose a situation below. Plan a dialogue between the characters and act it out.

1. **Aldo Leopold, the hunter.** They argue about killing the wolves.
2. **A male wolf, a female wolf.** They discuss where to move the den in order to save their cubs.
3. **Peter, his friend.** Peter explains Leopold's change from being willing to kill the wolves to protecting them.
4. **Two animals.** They talk about how to teach humans a lesson about helping nature.
5. **Leopold, his daughter.** He tells her she can't have a coat made out of wolf skins.
6. **Leopold, a conservation official.** They discuss how to save the forest and the animals.
7. **An ecologist, a politician.** The politician says he can not support ecology.

7. Silent Dialogue Through Writing

Draw a line down the middle of a piece of paper. With a partner, write a dialogue, silently. For example, one person writes something that Aldo Leopold would say, and passes the paper to his or her partner. The partner writes what Peter (or the hunter) might respond.

Chapter 14

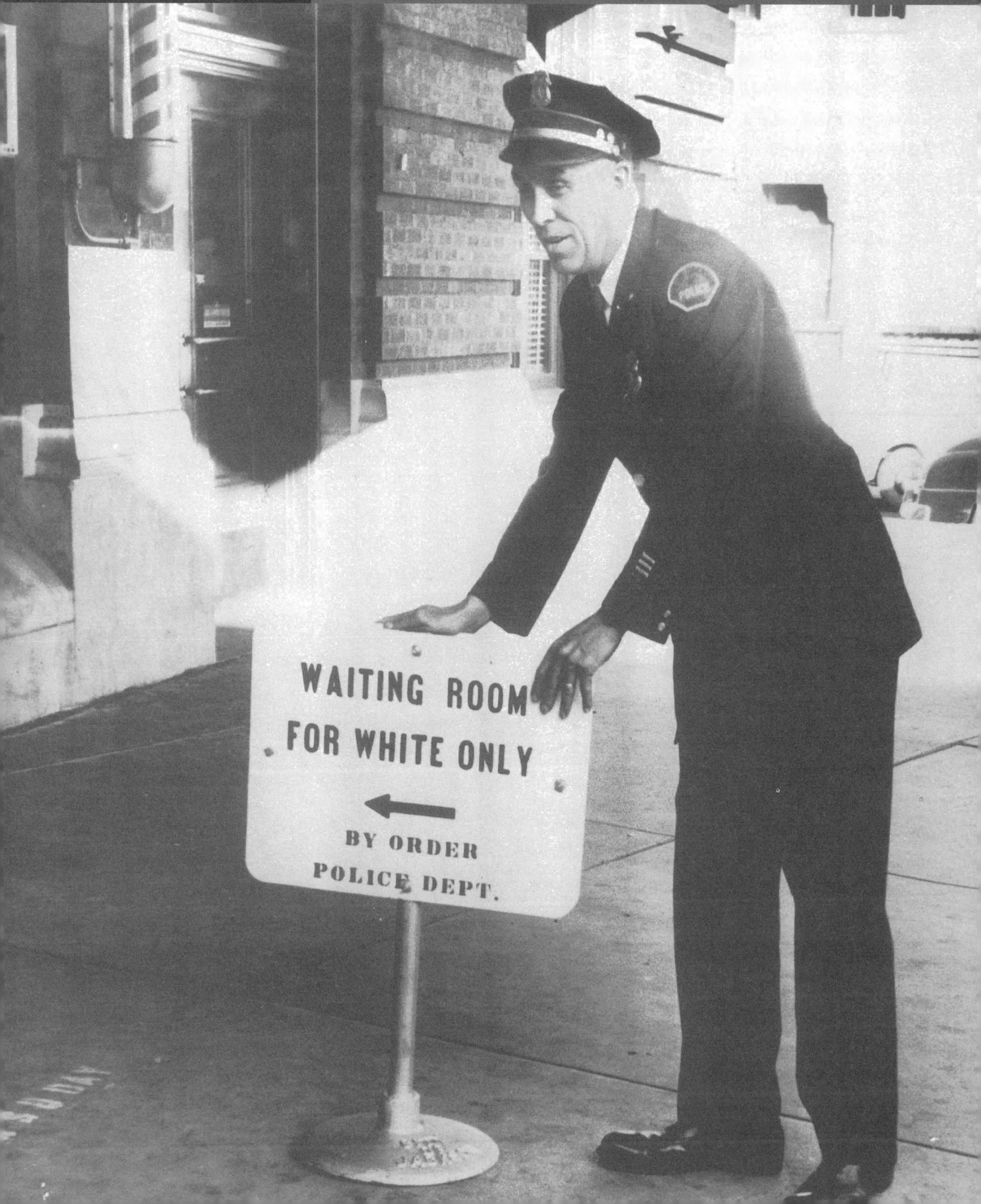

The
Bus Boycott

BEFORE YOU READ

Answer the following questions.

1. **Why is segregation bad?**

2. **What are civil rights?**

3. **Do all countries believe in basic rights for everyone?**

4. **What are basic rights? Why do you think they are basic?**

Words to Understand

Read the sentences. Discuss what the words in **boldface** mean.

Words About the Civil Rights Movement
1. The African-Americans worked hard to get their **civil rights.**
2. Many white people wanted to keep buses and schools **segregated.**
3. The blacks **boycotted** the buses because they believed the bus company was unfair.
4. Rosa Parks wouldn't **give up** her seat to a white person.

Legal Words
1. Because she **refused** to give up her seat, they arrested her and took her to jail.
2. She paid the **fine** but said she would **appeal** because it wasn't fair.
3. The Supreme Court said that segregation was **unconstitutional,** not allowed by the Constitution.
4. It is **illegal,** against the law, to treat people differently because of the color of their skin.

Everyday Words
1. It was normal, **common,** to see signs of segregation, such as "Whites Only."
2. Rosa Parks was **respected** by her community because she was a good person.
3. Martin Luther King, Jr., wanted to **avoid violence** during the boycott.
4. Using **carpools** means riding together, sharing a car.
5. A **rude** person is one who does impolite or discourteous actions.
6. **Y'all** is a southern way of saying you (plural).

Active Vocabulary Learning Activity

Work in pairs on a word or phrase your teacher gives you. Try to show or illustrate it. For example, if your phrase is "shoot arrows," you can say the phrase and at the same time make the physical motion of "shooting an arrow." If you wish, you can also make some gesture or facial expression related to the vocabulary.

Finally, repeat the word or the phrase and action with the class. Here are the words to use in this story:

boycott, segregate, respect, avoid violence, give up, refuse, rude.

At the time of this story, the South was **segregated:** schools, restaurants, movie theaters, even water fountains. "Whites only" was a **common** sign. On buses, white people sat in the front, and blacks sat in the back. If the white seats were filled, and a white person got on the bus, the driver would tell the blacks to stand so that the white person could sit down. Sometimes bus drivers didn't even allow black people to walk through the front part of the bus. They had to pay the driver in the front, get off, and reenter through the back door. Rosa Parks, a 42-year-old African-American, could remember stepping off the bus after paying and having it drive away, leaving her at the bus stop. Because of this injustice, she joined a group called the National Association for the Advancement of Colored People (NAACP). This group worked to win rights for black Americans. She became the secretary for the Alabama branch of the NAACP. The president of this organization was E. D. Nixon.

"We Shall Overcome", an old Negro Spiritual, became the unofficial anthem of the Civil Rights Movement.

We shall overcome
We shall overcome
We shall overcome
  some day

Refrain:
Oh deep in my heart
I do believe
We shall overcome
  some day

We are not afraid
We are not afraid
We are not afraid today
We'll walk hand in hand
We'll walk hand in hand
We'll walk hand in hand
  some day
We shall live in peace
We shall live in peace
We shall live in peace
  some day
The truth will make
  us free
The truth will make
  us free
The truth will make
  us free some day

The Bus Boycott

That Special Moment

Sometimes good things come out of bad. This is true about something that happened in Montgomery, Alabama, in 1955.

On Thursday, December 1, 1955, Rosa Parks got on a bus to go home after work. "Oh," she thought, "the driver is that **rude** man, James Blake, the driver
5 who left me standing on the sidewalk a few years ago." She paid her money and sat down. She didn't know that the most important moment of her life was coming.

After a few stops a white man got on the bus. Blake, seeing that all the seats for white passengers were filled, told the black people in Rosa's row to stand and
10 **give up** the row so that the white man could sit down. No one stood up.

"**Ya'll** make it light on yourselves and let me have those seats," Blake said. Three of the people in the row stood up, but Rosa didn't. She had decided that it was time to sit. She had paid for her seat. It was not fair to make her stand and give up her seat.

15 "Get up, woman. You have no right to this seat," the driver shouted.

"I will not get up," said Rosa Parks.

"I'm going to call the police, and they will arrest you."

"Go ahead," she said.

Rosa is Put in Jail

Rosa Parks **refused** to move.
20 Two policemen came and arrested Rosa. She was put in jail. E. D. Nixon came to the police station and paid bail money of $100 so that she could go home.

Rosa Parks was treated like a criminal for refusing to give up her seat.

SOURCE: The Granger Collection

"Rosa, are you willing to fight against paying the fine?" asked Nixon.

"Yes, I'm ready to fight," said Rosa Parks.

25   "People **respect** you. If you fight against the law that says that whites and blacks must sit in different parts of the bus, our people will support you," he said.

"Maybe we will be able to change things," she said.

Her husband, Raymond, said, "Rosa, I'm afraid some white people might
30 kill you."

"I'm sorry, Raymond, I've already decided." She had decided at the moment she refused to give up her seat.

There was already a group, the Women's Political Council, with a plan to stop riding buses. Nixon met with the local black ministers. The plan: all black
35 people would stop riding the buses on Monday morning. If they could not sit as the whites could, they would not ride at all. They would **boycott** the buses.

The Boycott Starts

One of the ministers was Martin Luther King, Jr. He was chosen to lead the boycott. On that Sunday in churches all over Montgomery, the ministers told their people about Rosa Parks and how she had refused to give up her seat.
40 They asked the people to boycott the buses on Monday.

The next morning the buses were almost empty. Only the white people rode them. Rosa Parks went to the courthouse. She said, "I'll pay the fine now for disobeying the bus driver, but I want to **appeal** this fine."

Her lawyer, Fred Gray, said "The law is unjust, and should be thrown out."

45   When Gray and Rosa Parks came out of the courthouse, a crowd of people cheered the brave woman.

Dr. Martin Luther King, Jr. became nationally famous as a leader of the boycott.

Monday night, Martin Luther King, Jr. gave a speech at a special church meeting. Several thousand people came. He said, "I want us to work together and **avoid violence.** The right way to fight hatred is with love, not with
50 hatred."

The boycott leaders met with the bus company. The blacks said, "We want to change the law forcing blacks to give up their seats to white people. And the bus company should hire some black drivers."

The bus company and the city said, "We refuse to change anything."

Illegal and Unconstitutional

55 Black people in Montgomery walked to work. They also organized **carpools** to get people to work. They used horses, mule carts, bicycles, even funeral hearses. But most of all, they walked.

For over a year, the black people of Montgomery refused to ride the buses. Many white people were angry. They blamed the black leaders for all the
60 trouble.

The Kings' house was bombed. He rushed home. His house was burning. "Where's my wife? my daughter? Are they hurt?"

"Reverend King, they were home, but they're all right. They weren't hurt," said a neighbor.
65 Finally, in January 1957, 14 months after the boycott started, Rosa's case was settled by the U.S. Supreme Court, the highest court in the nation. It ruled that Montgomery's segregation laws were **unconstitutional.**

The court said that segregated buses were unfair to African-American people and that it was **illegal** to treat people differently because of the color of their skin.

70

The day after the segregation laws changed, Rosa Parks rode the bus. She was happy to take a seat in the front row. This case showed that African-Americans could stand together and win their rights.

The Civil Rights Movement was born. Big things start small.

≈

Importance

The Montgomery bus boycott was a battle for civil rights. Rosa Parks became a symbol for the cause. She is called the "mother" of the Civil Rights Movement. Martin Luther King, Jr., became famous during this boycott. King believed in the nonviolent civil disobedience that Mahatma Gandhi had used against the British in India.

Focus on the Story

1. Understand the Story

Find out. Read the question. Find the answer in the story. Write it on the line.

> **Example:** Where does this story take place?
> It takes place in Montgomery, Alabama.

1. What does *segregation* mean? _____

_____

2. Why didn't Rosa Parks give up her seat in the bus to a white person? _____

_____

3. How did the African-Americans fight back against the bus segregation? _____

_____

4. What did Martin Luther King, Jr., do to help the boycott? _____

_____

5. What happened after 14 months of the boycott? _____

_____

6. What was another important right that African-Americans won in the 1950s? _____

_____

Until the mid 1950s, black children and white children in the South did not go to school together. The black children went to separate "colored schools." These schools had little money to pay teachers, or buy books. Schools had always been segregated. Many people started fighting the school segregation laws. In the 1950s the NAACP presented a case against segregated schools to the U. S. Supreme Court. The justices made a ruling in 1954. They said that separate schools for black and white children were unfair to black children. Integration of the schools began. This was a major victory for the Civil Rights Movement.

2. Practice Vocabulary

Choose the word or definition that is closest in meaning to the word(s) in **boldface.**

respected	common	rude	refused to
unconstitutional	illegal	blamed	

1. The court said that segregation on buses was **against the law.**
2. It was **usual** to see the "white only" sign all over the south.
3. Rosa Parks was **admired** by the black people of Montgomery.
4. Segregation was **against the Constitution** after 1957.
5. Rosa **would not** give up her seat to the white man.
6. The whites **criticized** the black leaders for the boycott.
7. The bus driver was **discourteous.**

3. Understand the Characters' Problems

Read about Parks' problem and her solution; then fill in the missing problem or solution for the other characters.

CHARACTER	PROBLEM	SOLUTION
Rosa	1. Told to move by driver	1. She refuses to move.
Nixon	2. Wants to test the segregation laws of Montgomery	2. _____ _____
Bus Driver	3. Must keep whites and blacks segregated	3. _____ _____
Black people of Montgomery	4. _____ _____	4. They boycott in the buses
Martin Luther King, Jr.	5. Wants to avoid violence	5. _____ _____

4. Talk About It

1. Why was the South segregated? Can you give any reasons?
2. Is there any place in the world that is segregated now?
3. What can be done to increase tolerance among people?
4. Can tolerance be taught?
5. Describe prejudice and what it does to people.

5. Write What You Think

1. Write a summary of this story. Add other things you know about segregation and civil rights.
2. Write a letter from a black person in Montgomery during the boycott to a friend in another city.
3. Write a dialog between a white person and a black person during this time.
4. Write a newspaper article about Rosa Parks and what she did.

6. Play the Part

Choose a situation below. Plan a dialogue between the characters and act it out.
1. **Parks, bus driver James Blake.** He wants her to get up. She doesn't want to.
2. **Parks, the judge.** He wants her to pay the fine. She says she wants to appeal the ruling.
3. **Rosa, Raymond.** He wants her to give up the fight against segregation. She says no.
4. **Martin Luther King, Jr., the town mayor.** The mayor tells him to stop the boycott. He says no.
5. **King, Nixon, the mayor, the bus company owner.** They all disagree.
6. **King, his wife.** After the bombing, she is afraid and wants to move away. He says no.

7. Story Theater

1. Work with a group of students.
2. Choose a section of the story with the class.
3. Read the section with your group. With your group decide which role you will play. If possible, change everything to conversation. Feel free to change the description to conversation. Choose any props you wish.
4. Practice your section for 15–20 minutes with your group.
5. Perform your story for the class. Try to make the story theater flow from one part to the next.

Chapter 15

Protesting the Vietnam War

BEFORE YOU READ

Answer the following questions.

1. **What do you know about the Vietnam War?**

2. **What do you know about the Cold War between Western nations and the Russian bloc (group)?**

Words to Understand

Read the sentences. Discuss what the words in **boldface** mean.

Words About the Vietnam War

1. In the 1960s people around the world **protested** the Vietnam War.
2. Americans became **horrified** about how many women and children were killed.
3. Others were afraid of the spread of **communism,** calling communists the **Reds.**
4. Some of those who supported the government, cried **"My country, right or wrong."**
5. In most parts of the world, the West's struggle against communism was a **Cold War,** but in Vietnam, it was "hot" with guns, shooting, people **bleeding.**
6. The **Viet Cong** were the Vietnamese soldiers in south Vietnam who were supported by north Vietnam in their fight against the American-supported southern Vietnamese.

Words About Protesting

1. Many young men ran away to Canada so that they would not be **drafted** into the army.
2. Two sisters had many **arguments** about the war.
3. If you ran away from the draft, you might be called a **traitor.**
4. In the 1960s, long-haired people were often called **"Hippies."**

Words About Emotion

1. The mother **begged** her son not to join the Army.
2. I **held back** the tears. I didn't want him to see me cry.
3. He was **amazed** that she still loved him after all those years.

Active Vocabulary Learning Activity

Work in pairs on a word or phrase your teacher gives you. Try to show or illustrate it. For example, if your phrase is "shoot arrows," you can say the phrase and at the same time make the physical motion of "shooting an arrow." If you wish, you can also make some gesture or facial expression related to the vocabulary.

Finally, repeat the word or the phrase and action with the class.
Here are the words to use in this story:

> horrified, protest, beg, swooped down, argument, held back,
> amazed, bleeding.

*B*y 1967 President Lyndon Johnson had sent 525,000 Americans to fight in Vietnam. Why did America fight in Vietnam? It is hard to understand why the United States was willing to lose 50,000 soldiers and spend billions of dollars a year in a 10-year unwinnable war 7,000 miles from its border. Five U.S. presidents poured money and men into this small country. Why? After World War II, the United States, along with other nations, focused on stopping the spread of communism. This period is called the **Cold War.** Communism was taking hold in Asia, and the U.S. government tried to stop it by taking a stand in Vietnam, but by 1967 television was bringing violent pictures of this war into America's living rooms. The image of the bombing of Vietnamese villages **horrified** millions of Americans and raised the voice of **protest** throughout the land. However, the majority of Americans supported President Lyndon Johnson, taking the traditional view, **"My country, right or wrong."** They thought that people who spoke against the war were hurting the boys fighting in Vietnam. This division gave the country its most serious domestic crisis since the Civil War of 1861. This story is told by a woman about her family's experience of the Vietnam War.

President Johnson discussed the Vietnam War on television.

SOURCE: The Granger Collection

Protesting the Vietnam War

Story of Two Sisters

"Nancy, you have to support your country," my sister Margaret told me for the fiftieth time. "If we don't care about Vietnam, your son Steve died for nothing."

"Margaret, I can support my country, but I can't support this war," I said. "Steve died because he was in the wrong place, 7,000 miles from home, fight-
5   ing an unwinnable war."

"If you think that, why did you let him go?" asked Margaret.

Here we were, cooking in the kitchen, having this **argument** again.

"As if anyone can stop an 18-year-old from doing what he wants to do and thinks is right—and I thought it was right at the time. I thought it was **my**
10 **country, right or wrong,** but I've changed. I don't believe we should be fighting in a Vietnamese civil war. We made a mistake sending our boys there."

"You're wrong. We must stop **communism.** It is spreading everywhere," said Margaret. "If Vietnam falls to the **Reds,** the next country will too. I'm glad my Sonny went to Vietnam to stop communism."

15 "And I'm glad he's back." I said. "Have you asked Sonny how he feels about the war? He's been in Vietnam; does he still think we're fighting for democracy over there?"

"No, I haven't asked him," said Margaret, and she stopped stirring the sauce and turned to me. "I just know he would feel bad if other young men fought
20 for his country and he didn't."

"Well, I'm glad Bob, my only son left, didn't go," I said. "He was right to run away to Canada, and he's not a **traitor.** We can't protect the whole world from communism. The Vietnamese should fight their own war; we can't do it for them."

A Hot Kitchen

25 "The kitchen is hot enough as it is without heating it up with words," said Jim, my husband, as he came in the room. "What's making you two sisters argue?"

"Oh, it's the same old story . . . the Vietnam War," Margaret said, carrying the salad to the dining room.

"Nancy, it's our 25th wedding **anniversary** party! Honey, don't argue
30 tonight, please," Jim asked.

Bob's girlfriend, Jill, came into the room, "Hello, everybody, may I help with anything?"

"Jill, how are you? Good to see you again," said Jim, giving Jill a hug.

Just then, a young man walked in behind Jill. I couldn't believe my eyes.
35 "Bob, you're here," I grabbed him.

"Mom, I couldn't stay away from your big night," said Bob.

"Son," said Jim, "don't you think it's dangerous? There are a lot of people here who know you fled the **draft** and went to Canada.

"Don't worry tonight, Dad," Bob said and turned to Jill, "Look who's here!
40 You look gorgeous," as he hugged her.

"Bob, you look so different . . . " said Jill, remembering that night two years before when she had **begged** Bob to let her go to Canada with him.

"It's my hair . . . it was down to my shoulders then, wasn't it? That long-haired look isn't safe for me now. I don't want to look like a **hippie.**"

45 I just watched the two of them, **amazed** that they could act so normal, as if life hadn't changed completely for us during these years. I **held back** my tears of joy at seeing Bob, and controlled my fear that the police could come to get him.

Fear and Celebration

"Bob, aren't you afraid? The police want you for **running away** from the **draft.**" Jill expressed my thoughts for me. Her eyes were full of light.
50 "I won't stay long. I couldn't miss my folks' anniversary. It's great to see the whole family together like this. Even Grandma is here," Bob said.

Margaret called us into the dining room for a picture.

The living room was filled with cousins from South Chicago. Smoke hung heavy near the ceiling. The camera kept flashing as someone took pictures of
55 everyone at this family reunion. The buzz of talk was everywhere, some voices outshouting others, but the laughter was louder than the talk. I could hear my mother's laughter from the corner.

Just then the room quieted down when Sonny's voice boomed with a story, "My pistol was empty. My M-16 was gone. My buddy was lying next to me
60 **bleeding.** Another buddy was already dead. There I was out in the middle of a rice field with dead Vietnamese women and children all around me. The enemy was shooting from the trees. Bang. Bang. Bang. Should I pick up my buddy and run for the river? I looked around, but there was no where to go. I thought I was a dead man." Sonny paused.

*B*efore the 1930s, Vietnam had been a colony of the French. Japan occupied it in World War II. After that war, the French fought for seven years to regain control, but they were defeated at Dien Bien Phu in 1954 by the Vietnamese led by their popular leader, Ho Chi Minh. The French pulled out but within a year, America was helping the Catholic noncommunist regime in the South led by Ngo Dinh Diem. In a predominantly Buddhist country, Diem had the support of the army and the Catholics (1 and 1/2 million people) in a country of 17 million. The situation was ripe for failure. In the 1960s, Vietnam became the hottest spot where communism and Western nations confronted each other. More bombs were dropped in Vietnam than during the whole of World War II.

SOURCE: The Granger Collection

U.S. soldiers were not prepared for the terrain they found in Vietnam.

65 "Then I heard a noise, 'Wop. Wop. Wop'— a helicopter. They saw me waving and **swooped down** to pick me up."

"Sonny," said Margaret, "We see enough of this on television."

"Then what happened? Then what happened?" asked the seven-year-old twins.

70 "They sent me home for some rest and relaxation," said Sonny with a laugh. He turned and saw Bob. His voice changed, "But hey, who's that over there with the short hair? I can't believe it. It's Bob. Let's hear your war stories. How's the war up in Canada?"

No Talking Now

No one said anything. Jim cleared his throat and started to say something, 75 but nothing came out. Margaret said, "Sonny, this is a party. Don't talk about the war now."

"I don't know why not. We're fighting a war in Vietnam. I'm serving my country. People are dying over there. I want to know how Bob, the 'peacenik,' feels about that," said Sonny.

80 Everyone was quiet. No more sounds of tinkling glasses, laughter, dancing, music.

"Sonny, I know that people have died there. I don't like it at all." Bob spoke softly. "My brother died there. I remember."

Still the room was quiet, as if we all were holding our breath. Even the 85 children stayed still. Sonny walked over to Bob, and everyone pulled back, not sure what would happen.

"What's going on?" said my mother from her big rocking chair in the corner. "Is this family falling apart? Families don't act like this."

I held my breath.

90 "OK, Grandma," Sonny said to my mother; then he turned to me, "I'm sorry, Aunt Nancy. I guess I forget sometimes." He turned to Bob and hugged him, "Hey, cousin."

"Sonny, it's so good to see you. Welcome home," said Bob.

"Maybe you're right about this crazy war, cousin; too many people are dying.
95 It's getting crazier all the time. Maybe we should pull out. Who knows?" said Sonny.

Bob hugged him back, tears glowing in his eyes. "Sonny, I hope you and I both stay home now," He stopped talking, unable to hide his tears.

"Hey, everybody," said Sonny, "Don't be so serious. It's party time."

100 Jill and I walked over to the two young men and put our arms around both of them.

Importance

Although the war was unpopular, it went on year after year. By the late 1960s, more Americans questioned why the United States was in Vietnam, and more people came to believe that the war was hopeless and that the United States was wrong to interfere and support a corrupt government that lacked popular support. However, the U.S. government had a hard time admitting that all that loss of life was for nothing. The presidents were afraid to lose more **prestige.** The protest movement was fed by mixed news: the government said we were winning in Vietnam, but the free press said we were losing. The American people felt that they were being misled, and even with all the wealth and firepower the United States could bring, the **Viet Cong** was still defeating the American forces everywhere.

1968 was a wild year, with protest all over the world: in Brazil, Italy, Poland, England, France, Japan, Mexico, and Czechoslovakia. Many countries were going through huge and violent change.

Focus on the Story

I. Understand the Story

With a partner, scan the Facts to Know, the story, and Importance sections for answers to these questions. (Scanning means to look over something for particular answers.)

1. How many Americans were sent to Vietnam by President Johnson?
2. How did Americans find out about the bombing of Vietnamese villages?
3. Which sister wants to support the war?
4. Which sister has a son who died in the Vietnam War?
5. Where did Bob go? Why does he have short hair now?
6. Who is telling the story about being in a rice field in Vietnam?
7. How do Sonny and Bob treat each other?
8. Who is the older lady who tells Sonny to stop hurting the family?
9. What was the name of the period when the Western countries tried to stop communism from spreading?
10. What other Western country fought against the Vietnamese before the United States did?
11. Was 1968 a difficult year in other countries? Why? Where?

2. Practice Vocabulary

Use these words to complete the sentences:

prestige   anniversary   amazed   swooped down
arguments   begged   traitor   protested

1. The helicopter came and _____ to pick up the soldier.

2. A _____ is someone who hurts his country.

3. The president feared loss of _____ over the war.

4. Many people _____ against the war for many years.

5. Bob came back home for his parents' 25th wedding _____ party.

6. Grandma was _____ that life goes on, through good and bad.

7. Nancy and Margaret disagreed, and had many _____ about the war.

8. Jill wanted to go with him; she _____ him to take her to Canada.

3. Make Inferences

To make an inference, we combine what we see and hear with what we already know (background knowledge) to make conclusions (inferences) about a character or situation in stories. More than one anwer could be right.

> **For example:** Make an inference about why Margaret supports the
> Vietnam War.
> Here are two possible answers:
> She really is afraid of communism taking over the world.
> She believes its important to support her country.

1. **Story of Two Sisters:** Make an inference about why Nancy hates the war.
2. **A Hot Kitchen:** Make an inference about Jill and Bob's relationship.
3. **Fear and Celebration:** Make an inference about the type of family this is.
4. **No One is Talking:** Make an inference about why everyone quiets down.

4. Talk About It

Discuss these questions with a partner or in a small group:
1. Was the Vietnam War immoral or bad? Support your answer with reasons.
2. Why did France fight in Vietnam?
3. Why did the United States fight in Vietnam?
4. What were the reasons that the United States could not defeat the Vietnamese?
5. Would you fight in an army in a war you did not believe was just? Why?
6. If not, give the reasons you would not. What would you do instead?

5. Write What You Think

1. Write a letter home from an American soldier in Vietnam.
2. Describe reasons either for (pro) or against (con) war, general or specific.
3. Write an answer for any of the questions in Section 4, on page 120.

6. Play the Part

Choose a situation below. Plan a dialogue between the characters and act it out.
1. **Nancy, Margaret.** They argue about the war.
2. **Bob, his father Jim.** Jim wants Bob to hurry back to Canada; Bob says no.
3. **Bob, Jill.** She wants to return to Canada with him; he wants to stay and protest the war.
4. **Bob, Sonny.** Bob tells Sonny the war is wrong. Sonny defends the war.
5. **Sonny, Margaret.** He argues against the Vietnam War; she supports the war.
6. **Grandmother, Bob, Sonny.** They discuss the war.

7. Geography Focus

Use the map below to answer the questions.
1. Trace a route from the United States to Vietnam by ship and by air.
2. Which countries border Vietnam?
3. Which country is north of Vietnam?
4. Which country is south of Vietnam?
5. Do any of these countries have communist governments now?

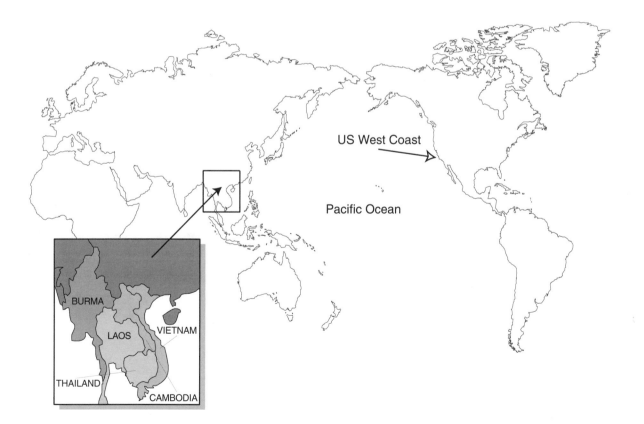

Index

Note: Numbers in parentheses indicate chapter numbers in which a form of the word is found.

fine (14)
flat plains (5)
fool's gold (5)
force (8)
fragment (5)
frenzied (5)
gallant (12)
give in (2)
give up (9), (11), (14)
glitters (5)
glory (6)
go back and forth (2)
going to pieces (11)
goodness gracious (6)
Goodwife, Goody, Goodman (3)
got to, get to (3)
Great Spirit (9)
greedy (3)
groups (13)
guilty (3)

H
habitat (14)
hammers (7)
handicapped (11)
hanged (3)
hard substance (1)
head man (7)
heavy things (9)
held back (15)
heroes (6)
hippie (15)
hired (7), (12)
home area (13)
homely (8)
horrified (15)
horror and misery (6)
hostile (9)
hurrah (4)
hurricanes (10)
hush (4)

I
illegal (14)
imitated (3)
immediate release (8)
important (3)
indigenous (9)
industrial (6)
injustice (9)
inspiration (11), (15)

insult, insulted (4)
interdependent (14)
interrupting (2)
invaded, invading (4)
invalid (15)

J, K, L
jail (3)
just in case (4)
keep order (10)
keep the promises (9)
kidnapped (2)
know (3)
know-it-all (10)
lay track (7)
line (9)
locked away (7)

M
making people behave (10)
mansion (4)
mayor (6)
medicine man (9)
messenger (4)
metal (1)
mica (5)
minister (3)
mischievous (12)
mistress (3)
Mormon (5)
mourning (9)
must be sacrificed (4)
my country, right or wrong (13)

N, O
nailed to the wall (4)
naked (3)
nanny (2)
natives (1)
natural resources (14)
never had enough (3)
nightmares (6)
nitroglycerine (7)
noise (10)
not proud (9)
on her own behalf (8)
operate a camera (12)
opponent (8)
opportunity (5)
outburst (11)
overpopulated (13)
overrated (5)

P, Q
packs (14)
paralyzed (11)
pay attention (12)
permission (6)
plantations (6)
polio (11)
portrait (4)
praying for (2)
precious (4)
predators (13)
prejudice(d) (7)
prestige (15)
pride (6)
private property (4)
prize (6)
protested (15)
pull (myself) together (11)
Puritan (3)
quit (7)

R
raised their clubs (2)
recognize (3)
recovered (11)
Reds (15)
refugees (10)
refused (14)
relatives (10)
relief (10)
religious (10)
remedy (11)
resourceful (12)
respect (2), (14)
retire (11)
retreat(ing) (5)
revenge (9)
Richter scale (10)
ridiculed (8)
ridiculous (8)
right(s) (8), (9)
risk (12)
roar (10)
robe (2)
rude (14)
rumble (10)
run away (2), (15)